FOCUS
PLAYS THREE

Jon Fosse

PLAYS THREE

MOTHER AND CHILD
SLEEP MY BABY SLEEP
AFTERNOON
BEAUTIFUL
DEATH VARIATIONS

Translated by May-Brit Akerholt

methuen | drama

LONDON • NEW YORK • OXFORD • NEW DELHI • SYDNEY

METHUEN DRAMA
Bloomsbury Publishing Plc
50 Bedford Square, London, WC1B 3DP, UK
1385 Broadway, New York, NY 10018, USA
29 Earlsfort Terrace, Dublin 2, Ireland

BLOOMSBURY, METHUEN DRAMA and the Methuen Drama logo
are trademarks of Bloomsbury Publishing Plc

First published in Great Britain by Oberon Books 2004
Reprinted in 2011
This edition published by Bloomsbury Methuen Drama 2024

ISBN: PB: 978-1-3505-1440-9

Series: Oberon Modern Playwrights

Printed and bound in Great Britain

To find out more about our authors and books visit www.bloomsbury.com
and sign up for our newsletters.

Contents

MOTHER AND CHILD
(Mor og barn)

Characters

THE MOTHER

THE BOY

A living room

THE MOTHER
    It's really good to see you
    It's been a long time
    I hardly ever
    see you
    The Boy is a little happy, a little embarrassed
    Either you are away
    or I am
    We're hardly ever in the same place
    at the same time
    She laughs shortly
    Hardly ever
    But now
    She moves to him and puts her hand on his shoulder and
    shakes him a little
    we're together
    And not too soon either
    And I've just come back from England
    I was there for that
    Looks at him
    But you know that
    I've already told you
    And now we're finally together
    I'm glad you found the time to drop in
    Have you been here before
    I mean
    Here
    She looks around
    where I live now

THE BOY
    No

THE MOTHER
    No of course
    you haven't
    I know that
    when I think about it

This is where I've lived
for many years
already
It's too bad
It was none too soon
So you took
a trip to Oslo
What are you doing here
by the way
She doesn't wait for an answer
Yes it's good that we
finally get to see each other
We see each other
so rarely
Hardly ever
But then we do live in different parts of the country
I live here in Oslo
in the capital
Forced laughter
while you live over there
on the west coast
among fjords and mountains
Short pause
I often long to go back
but somehow I never get around to it
Fjords and mountains
However you've been staying abroad a lot
you as well
We live in different parts of the country
And besides we're both
often abroad
so it isn't so strange that we don't see
a lot of each other
Look at you you're
a grown man now
Looks at him with satisfaction
Well well how big you've grown

She laughs
A grown-up man
I must admit I'm proud
when I think about it
to have a grown-up son
And then you're my only child
And I hardly ever see you
Short pause
Really it's too bad
I live here alone
and have a son I hardly ever see

THE BOY
Yes
It's come to that

THE MOTHER
We should've met more often
It's just so difficult to make it happen
Still
We could've met each other
Now and then
if not so often
But you're busy with your life
I with mine
She laughs
We struggle on
Remembers something
But you've just been sitting for your exams
You said you'd just
finished your exams
Well how did it go
Did it go well
Did you do well
What was it like
abroad
where you were studying
Tell me
Please tell me

13

THE BOY
  It went well

THE MOTHER
  You got good grades

THE BOY
  Not too bad
  But not too good
  either

THE MOTHER
  But that's not really important
  What's important
  Laughs
  Well you tell me
  Short pause
  We seem to have come to
  the big questions already

THE BOY
  Yes that's a big question

THE MOTHER
  And I'm not very good at
  the big questions
  She laughs
  Not anymore
  In my youth
  perhaps
  but not
  anymore
  No
  No not anymore

THE BOY
  Who said that

THE MOTHER
  No one would say it
  it's just

the way it is
I don't care so much anymore
about the big questions
I don't think so much
any more
about life and death
and that sort of thing
I get along

THE BOY
Yes you get along with less

THE MOTHER
I suppose I do
Short pause
And that's for the best
because I'm
just a woman
And women should leave
big questions alone
She laughs
No honestly
I get so depressed
From thinking
I get so sad
when I think about
the way things are
I suppose that's
how it is
She looks at him
Yes that's true

THE BOY
Yes

THE MOTHER
Listen

THE BOY
Yes

THE MOTHER
>Listen
>*She laughs*
>I'm glad to have a son
>I mean
>I'm glad you're a boy
>and not a girl
>*She laughs*

THE BOY
>Yes

THE MOTHER
>I mean
>I
>I've always liked men better than women
>*She laughs*
>But you can't say things like that
>All the same it's true
>Even if I've always been
>you know a feminist
>but you can't say things like that any more
>It's like saying you're not keeping up with the times
>But I've always been you know
>a feminist

THE BOY
>Yes
>Yes I know that

THE MOTHER
>Yes always been one
>not because I like women so much
>On the contrary
>I've been one because I
>between you and me
>*Laughs*
>well because I
>often

if not always
of course
simply can't stand women
in any case there are a lot of women
I don't like
if I may say
I'd like to tell you something

THE BOY
No don't
Short pause
But how are you going
Are you doing alright

THE MOTHER
Yes
Short pause
You could say that
I can't complain
But I'm pretty busy
At work
I mean

THE BOY
Lots of travelling
You're often abroad

THE MOTHER
Yes quite a bit
But I'm doing alright

THE BOY
And any other news

THE MOTHER
Any other news
No nothing in particular
At least I can't think
of anything
just now
at least

17

But I'm doing alright
I can't complain

THE BOY
No

THE MOTHER
But of course I'm pretty
busy
there's a lot to do
yes

THE BOY
Yes

THE MOTHER
Yes you could say that

THE BOY
But it's a while since you've been
to the West Coast

THE MOTHER
Yes it's been years
I don't think I've been there
since my mother died
since I was there
for her funeral
Short pause
No I haven't
Yes time just disappears

THE BOY
Yes

THE MOTHER
Time disappears
And now
Looks at him
you're a grown man
already

I can't believe it

THE BOY
Yes

THE MOTHER
Smiles
It's unbelievable
So you didn't want to hear
what I wanted to tell you
She laughs
No I'm sure it's just as well
Pause. She looks at him
But it's such a long time since
I've seen you
We should've seen
each other more often
Remember when you were a little boy
and we were fishing out on the fjord

THE BOY
Yes when you came to stay

THE MOTHER
Yes
you and I and my dad
your granddad
That great rowboat he had
remember that
Remember
when we went fishing
in summer
All the fish we caught
Often the whole boat was filled
with fish
Remember when we fished herring
Remember that
And we caught trout
Salmon

And we lit a bonfire
out there on the reef
Do you remember

THE BOY
Yes that was good
I remember

THE MOTHER
Yes we spent some time together
if not very much
when you grew up

THE BOY
Yes

THE MOTHER
It's not how it should have been
However
Short pause
everything was so difficult
I was going to university
was going to become something
I couldn't just
settle down
in that backwater
with a kid
alone with a kid
I was so young you see
It was all so bewildering
Yes
Pause
But we did OK
both you and I
right

THE BOY
Yes
Pause
My grandparents

were good to me
Dad too

THE MOTHER
Yes
Pause
I didn't know
what to do
It was so

THE BOY
Yes I understand

THE MOTHER
And my parents gave you
a good home
didn't they

THE BOY
Yes they did
Yes I've been fine

THE MOTHER
Yes
But

THE BOY
But that's not how it should've been
Is that what you want to say
Why not

THE MOTHER
No I don't know
Pause

THE BOY
No

THE MOTHER
But I had to
get an education
That's what I wanted

And there was nothing wrong
with that
The Boy shakes his head
No
What would have become of me
if I hadn't
got myself an education
But I did it
I got an education
That's what I did
And I made something of myself
too
A little loudly
Yes I made something of myself

THE BOY
Yes
And soon you'll be
I bet
a big boss

THE MOTHER
A little happier
Oh rubbish
Short pause
Me a big boss
no
I don't know
about that
She laughs
My first boss
She did nothing
Not a thing
And her decisions were always
the most unimaginative and bureaucratic
the most ineffective
I've ever been part of
in my whole life

as you know
I'm a sort of bureaucrat
too
It was absolutely awful
And she didn't like me
I don't look
She laughs
I don't look too bad
even if I'm not as young as I used to be
and have a big son
like you
Yes I have an almost

THE BOY
Oh well

THE MOTHER
Continues
grown-up son
But I've kept my looks
She poses for him
Don't you think I look good
She laughs
I'm still quite good-looking
Don't you think
There aren't many women my age
who look as good
as I do
She laughs
Or
No you shouldn't say things like that
to your own son

THE BOY
What happened

THE MOTHER
Continues
Oh yes

Her
No it didn't work at all
It couldn't work
Nothing got done
and the little that did get done
was all wrong

THE BOY
Yes

THE MOTHER
But it was unbearable
I nearly resigned
I
and many others
Nearly everyone in the department
nearly resigned
At least
Laughs
all the women
And me
she couldn't stand me
It's really true
I don't know what it was
but when she stood up
she smelled
She reeked
I don't know what the smell was
She laughs
That smell
Of course I know what it was
She laughs
Couldn't stand it
Short pause
It's important that women are in top management
positions
it's not that
I've always believed that
I don't mean to say

that women shouldn't be in top management positions
But that woman
Christ
Short pause
And you
I haven't seen you for ages
And you
She puts her hand on his shoulder, a little sentimentally
are my son

THE BOY
Did she resign

THE MOTHER
That woman
Yes she had to
Or all the others would've resigned
No I shouldn't say things like that
I'm a woman myself
I could even
Laughs a little
become boss
myself
After all I have
and that's not too bad
right
climbed the ranks
of the public service
I've done well
Looks at him
You can be proud
of me
She laughs
I'm a high-ranking employee
In the public service
Not bad that
I've done well
right

THE BOY
  Yes

THE MOTHER
  Yes really
  From the depths of the country side
  I've worked my way up
  I certainly have
  to a crucial position
  in the public service
  That's not too bad
  She laughs
  She has studied and worked
  her way up
  your mother
  from her grass roots
  she has worked her way up
  She worked and studied and struggled
  and kept climbing
  higher and higher
  till she got close to
  the real power
  Ha
  You have
  Coy
  quite a mum
  don't you
  An amazing mum
  you have
  From fjords and mountains
  right to the pinnacle of power
  or at least
  almost
  to the pinnacle of power
  Just below the pinnacle
  one could say
  at least
  I think I could say that

Short pause
That's how it is
She looks at him
But how are things with you
How are you going
Tell me
please
Did your exams go well
Tell me
And why are you in Oslo
Say something
Tell me

THE BOY
Oh yes everything's fine

THE MOTHER
And here in Oslo
You're
Pause. She seems to have remembered something
No it's terrible
Pause

THE BOY
Just say it

THE MOTHER
No it's nothing

THE BOY
OK

THE MOTHER
No I don't know
Short pause
Just forget it
Short pause
It was nothing

THE BOY
You just thought of something

27

THE MOTHER
Yes
As if to herself
No it's terrible

THE BOY
You shouldn't think about it then

THE MOTHER
But I should
Pause
I

THE BOY
Yes

THE MOTHER
No just forget it

THE BOY
Laughs a little
Yes alright
If that's what you want

THE MOTHER
It's nothing
Pause. Looks at her son
But it was good of you
to drop in and see me
It's been so long since
I've seen you
I hardly remember
when I saw you last
I know it's a long time ago
Questioningly
Wasn't it
at my mother's
funeral

THE BOY
I think it was

THE MOTHER
> It is
> really
> that long ago

THE BOY
> Yes I think it is

THE MOTHER
> Yes I think you're
> right
> *Pause. Looks at her son*
> It was dreadful
> her funeral
> I don't think I've quite recovered
> from it
> not
> yet
> Listen to me carrying on
> *She laughs*
> I don't know why I keep carrying on

THE BOY
> You're not carrying on

THE MOTHER
> But tell me
> How did your exams go
> Did you do well
> Tell me
> What are you doing in Oslo
> Tell me

THE BOY
> I did well

THE MOTHER
> *Laughs*
> You don't say much
> you're not exactly talkative

THE BOY
  No

THE MOTHER
  But that's how they are
  people from the West Coast

THE BOY
  No

THE MOTHER
  They're not

THE BOY
  No

THE MOTHER
  No
  Short pause
  Why do you keep saying no
  She laughs
  What do you mean by that
  No
  Why is no all you say
  Short pause
  You certainly don't talk much
  Wasn't it literature
  you studied there
  yes
  yes I know where you went to university
  you've told me
  it has simply slipped my mind
  in
  was it Dublin
  it was Ireland I know that
  Questioningly
  Dublin

THE BOY
  Galway
  That's where I studied literature

THE MOTHER
    Shakespeare and Homer
    and Beckett
    well Beckett for sure
    since it was Ireland
    And Joyce
    And Yeats

THE BOY
    Yes

THE MOTHER
    Yes
    As you can see I'm not
    a complete fool
    in matters of literature
    myself
    it's not that I've read
    all that much
    My reading is limited to
    She laughs
    bureaucratic transcripts
    these days
    Proceedings

THE BOY
    Yes

THE MOTHER
    And before Ireland
    you were in Germany
    just outside Stuttgart
    wasn't that where you were
    The Boy nods
    And you studied philosophy
    He nods again
    Yes philosophy

THE BOY
    Yes

31

THE MOTHER
Short laugh
No one could say
you talk too much
Short pause
All you can say
Short pause
is yes
No no no
Yes
Yes
Yes
Can't you tell me something
You must have had the odd experience
out there
in Ireland
in Germany
You must have something to talk about
surely

THE BOY
But it's so difficult
I can't just suddenly start talking
There has to be

THE MOTHER
Continues his sentence
a time and a place for it
Yes I know
Short pause
And this isn't
the time and the place for it
Because I keep carrying on
Womanfuss
Fuss fuss
She laughs. Looks at him
Look I'm sorry
I don't mean
To hurt anyone

THE BOY
   No

THE MOTHER
   Copies him
   No

THE BOY
   You mean

THE MOTHER
   Quickly
   I don't mean anything
   You don't either
   I'm sure
   She laughs

THE BOY
   No

THE MOTHER
   You don't mean anything
   And you only read these old
   male
   authors
   and philosophers
   Short pause

THE BOY
   Yes

THE MOTHER
   Well what do I know
   The Boy takes out a packet of cigarettes, lights one
   You smoke
   He nods
   It's not good for you
   but you know that
   He nods again

THE BOY
   Yes

THE MOTHER
   But you still smoke

THE BOY
   Nods
   I smoke
   yes
   But you've quit

THE MOTHER
   Yes
   Rather
   I smoke now and then
   but I'm not a smoker
   Short pause
   I managed to quit
   You haven't thought about quitting
   have you

THE BOY
   Shakes his head
   No

THE MOTHER
   You haven't
   Short pause
   Well
   But can I ask you something
   Short pause
   No it's nothing

THE BOY
   OK then
   But you can ask
   if you want to

THE MOTHER
   Do you hate women

THE BOY
>*Surprised*
>Do I hate women
>Why do you ask that

THE MOTHER
>*Laughs*
>Well you've never had a girlfriend

THE BOY
>No
>*Falters*

THE MOTHER
>I mean
>You haven't found
>a nice girl you'd like to be
>your girlfriend
>have you

THE BOY
>No unfortunately

THE MOTHER
>*Laughs, a little teasingly*
>No I suppose you're gay
>aren't you
>my little son
>my dearest only son is gay
>My gay son

THE BOY
>*A little cross*
>OK OK

THE MOTHER
>Aren't you

THE BOY
>Rather a sadist

THE MOTHER
> *As if shocked*
> A sexual sadist
> *Short pause*
> That sounds exciting
> Tell me
> tell me

THE BOY
> *Flippantly*
> You're my mother

THE MOTHER
> Exactly
> and that's why you
> can tell me everything
> *She laughs*
> I won't tell anyone
> No I wouldn't do that
> Or maybe I'll tell
> one of my friends
> My son's a masochist
> I'll whisper to her
> Not gay
> as I've told you before
> but a sadist
> a masochist
> *Short pause. She looks at him*
> But I suppose I too
> *She giggles*
> lean a bit that way
> so
> just between you and me
> No enough of this
> *Seemingly pulls herself together*
> I'm a public servant
> a female public servant
> who doesn't smoke
> Because smoking's not allowed

Short pause. Looks at the Boy
Can I have one of your cigarettes
He holds out his packet to her, she takes one
Do you have a light too
He gives her his lighter, she lights the cigarette, gives him back the lighter. She pulls deeply on the cigarette a few times, looks at the Boy
Smoking's a health hazard

THE BOY
It sure is

THE MOTHER
You're loosening up
Keep going

THE BOY
No

THE MOTHER
Yes keep going

THE BOY
Alright
I
I just wanted to know
Dad said

THE MOTHER
A little scared
What do you want to know

THE BOY
No it's nothing

THE MOTHER
Yes
Quickly
But you mentioned your father
Have you spoken to him
Where is he
Is he alright

THE BOY
Yes

THE MOTHER
So he's fine

THE BOY
Yes

THE MOTHER
Does he still
live with this
well this
I've never met her
But you know her

THE BOY
Yes

THE MOTHER
Did they have any more children

THE BOY
Yes two

THE MOTHER
They've got two small children
have they really

THE BOY
Yes

THE MOTHER
And they've got a daughter too
She's almost grown up

THE BOY
Yes
Short pause
But dad told me

THE MOTHER
A little scared
Yes
Yes they've had their hands full

THE BOY
Yes

THE MOTHER
You've got
three half siblings
You may not have any siblings
But at least
You've got
that

THE BOY
Interrupts
Dad's doing fine

THE MOTHER
I haven't seen him
for many years
We were quite young of course
when we met
And we didn't live together
for all that long
either
Only a few months

THE BOY
And you haven't seen him
since

THE MOTHER
I have

THE BOY
Oh yes you saw him as well
at grandma's funeral

THE MOTHER
Yes

THE BOY
>Why are you asking about him

THE MOTHER
>Oh I don't know
>anyway
>why's that so strange
>We have

THE BOY
>Yes you have a child together
>Me

THE MOTHER
>That's right

THE BOY
>Yes

THE MOTHER
>I'm just asking
>I'm just wondering
>how he is
>*Short pause*
>Did you enjoy growing up with him

THE BOY
>I've got nothing against my dad
>Besides

THE MOTHER
>Yes I know you lived for a long time
>with my parents
>if that's what you were about to say

THE BOY
>He's a good man
>Dad

THE MOTHER
>*A little petulant*
>And I'm not

THE BOY
> *Looks at her, laughs a little*
> Yes

THE MOTHER
> What am I then

THE BOY
> No

THE MOTHER
> You don't know

THE BOY
> No

THE MOTHER
> No no
> Yes yes
> Shall I tell you what I am
> What you would like to say
> if you dared to
> Shall I tell you
> You wanted to say
> You're horny
> and thick
> *She laughs*

THE BOY
> *A little resigned*
> No

THE MOTHER
> You wanted to say horny
> at least

THE BOY
> I didn't

THE MOTHER
> I am horny
> you wanted to say
> But your father isn't horny

41

not him
Or rather
he is the one who should be
he's a man
so
he's supposed to be
horny
that is
I'm a woman
and I'm not supposed to be horny
I'm supposed to sit
She squeezes her thighs together
with my thighs squeezed tight
My mother always told me that
Keep your legs together
she said
She laughs
A women should sit with her thighs squeezed tight
and she should be surrounded
by horny men
like your father
But I mustn't be horny
I've just got to be there
so that men like your father
can have their appetites gratified

THE BOY
Anyway

THE MOTHER
Yes
Anyway
The Mother laughs
Anyway
You know
My mother always said that
Anyway
You say it just

the way she used to
You sound like my mother
My grassroots mother
with minimal education
but with fire in her eyes
and a big faith
in herself
and in her Lord Jesus Christ
Short pause
Imagine you
sounding like her

THE BOY

Why do you say that
What do you want

THE MOTHER

I don't want anything
Long pause
But why can't we
Long pause
Well how was it
over there in Ireland
In Germany
Why don't you tell me a few things
What are you doing in Oslo
I am
She laughs
despite everything your mother
Short pause
But you know that
Short laugh
Because you've come to see me
Looks around
here at my place
You
Looks at him
have come here

Finally you came
I've lived here
for many years
and finally you came
of your own free will
to visit me

THE BOY
I haven't been
in Oslo
for many years

THE MOTHER
Yes
You don't need to apologise

THE BOY
No

THE MOTHER
I know just what it's like
But you might have been coming
here to Oslo
without looking me up
or
The Boy shrugs his shoulders. Short pause
Yes well
But it isn't so strange
either
that we don't meet
so often
Because you've been studying abroad
and lived most of your life
over there on the West Coast
with your father
and that woman
the one he lives with
she's got to put up with a lot of things
She laughs
she must be easy to please

44

THE BOY
  Calmly
  Oh well
  Pause

THE MOTHER
  Look, I'm sorry
  I don't mean to hurt anyone
  I'm just chatting on
  talk talk talk

THE BOY
  Yes I should've come
  to see you earlier
  I know that
  But

THE MOTHER
  Yes I know what it's like
  No need to apologise
  I
  Well I didn't visit
  my mother very often
  either
  when truth be told
  Almost never
  I should have
  but I didn't

THE BOY
  And now it's too late

THE MOTHER
  Yes
  Pause
  But let's
  Short pause
  Why don't we
  Yes

Why don't we talk about something else
You read a lot

THE BOY
Yes

THE MOTHER
I haven't got much time
to read
myself

THE BOY
But when you were a student

THE MOTHER
We read what we were supposed to read
The syllabus

THE BOY
Yes
Just the syllabus

THE MOTHER
No of course not
We read a lot of stuff

THE BOY
Yes

THE MOTHER
But what do you read
then

THE BOY
Oh all sorts of things

THE MOTHER
Yes I suppose
Short pause
So you don't like women
do you

THE BOY
What makes you say that

THE MOTHER
No
I don't know
I just have a feeling that's all
Just a feeling
I imagine
No
I don't know
But they just sit there
these women
She laughs
they just sit there with their breasts
jiggling their breasts
and feel oh so important
oblivious to the fact they've got breasts
Isn't that what you
feel about women
Women have breasts

THE BOY
What do you want

THE MOTHER
Suddenly
I too have breasts
She sticks out her breasts
Big breasts
pretty big
even
great breasts
She looks down on her breasts
Don't you agree
I've got great breasts
At least that's what you thought once
Childish voice
Go bye-byes on mummy's boob

That's what you said
And if I didn't let you
you'd start to cry
You often slept on my breast
you did
although it'd give me a backache
Go bye-byes on mummy's boob
Woke up in the morning with a sore back
And it

THE BOY
Interrupts
Yes I know
that it was bloody awful to give birth to me
if that's what you
were going to say

THE MOTHER
Yes
Horrible
it was
And I decided
bugger it

THE BOY
How many times
are you going to tell me
that story

THE MOTHER
Oh yes I decided
Looks at him
listen to me
that I would never give birth to any more kids
Never

THE BOY
I'm listening
I'm listening

THE MOTHER
>*Smiles at him*
>Go bye-byes on mummy's boob
>*Pause.*
>*She goes and puts her arms around him, holds him tightly, lets*
>*him go, looks at him, sighs*
>Can't we stop this
>I gave birth to you
>Go bye-byes on mummy's boob
>*She smiles at him. Short pause*
>It was good of you
>to come and see me
>We live
>We are what we are
>Man woman
>Mother son

THE BOY
>Mother and child
>*Short pause, looks at his mother*
>Dad said

THE MOTHER
>Come on say it

THE BOY
>No

THE MOTHER
>*Becomes a little scared*
>Yes

THE BOY
>No it's nothing

THE MOTHER
>Come on tell me

THE BOY
>No nothing

THE MOTHER
  Tell me

THE BOY
  That you

THE MOTHER
  Scared
  Yes that I

THE BOY
  No it's nothing
  Pause. Then quickly
  But you didn't
  even though Dad did
  want me to be born
  Dad said that
  I thought that now
  yes

THE MOTHER
  Yes

THE BOY
  I don't know
  but
  Long pause

THE MOTHER
  What can I say

THE BOY
  So we both know
  both of us
  I mean

THE MOTHER
  Yes we do

THE BOY
  Yes it's true

THE MOTHER
Yes
Pause

THE BOY
Looks at his mother
Perhaps I shouldn't have asked
Short pause
But it's a bit strange to think
that if it hadn't been for that committee
I wouldn't have been here
Perhaps it would have been for the best
if I hadn't been here
I mean

THE MOTHER
No don't say that

THE BOY
Yes
If it was up to you
I wouldn't have been born
No I won't say it
It would've been for the best
Don't take it the wrong way
I'm not accusing you
Looks at his mother
Look I'm sorry
Look I shouldn't have

THE MOTHER
It's alright
Short pause. On the verge of tears
I understand
You hate me
And that's
fair enough

THE BOY
I don't hate you

THE MOTHER
You hate me

THE BOY
No

THE MOTHER
You don't hate me

THE BOY
No I don't hate you
Pause
Or perhaps I hate you
and therefore I hate all women
Perhaps
Laughs. Pause. Looks at his mother
No I don't hate you
And I don't hate women
I just
If I hate something
it isn't you
but
yes
perhaps
perhaps I hate
Interrupts himself
No I don't know

THE MOTHER
No

THE BOY
Perhaps you should have
Stops
Yes I mean that
I shouldn't have existed
He laughs
It would've been for the best
I mean that

THE MOTHER
> *Suddenly very sad*
> No don't say that
> *Short pause*
> I don't know
> I don't
> *Long pause*
> But everything's so different
> from what it was then
> Nothing's the same
> You'd never understand
> how it was
> I can't tell you
> how it was
> *Pause*

THE BOY
> *Laughs*
> But I'm going to kill myself in any case

THE MOTHER
> Don't say that

THE BOY
> So you might as well
> *Short pause*
> And I'll tell you

THE MOTHER
> Yes

THE BOY
> No it's nothing

THE MOTHER
> Just tell me

THE BOY
> No forget it
> *Long pause*

No perhaps I should
Goes towards the door

THE MOTHER
Looks after him
Did you come
when you finally decided to visit me
just to make me say
that I

THE BOY
Turns towards his mother
No no

THE MOTHER
No don't go
Stay for a while
Couldn't we
Yes
We don't have to
It's been so long since I've seen you
Couldn't we
Tell me what you're doing in Oslo
Please don't go
not yet

THE BOY
No

THE MOTHER
Stay for a while

THE BOY
Well if you want me to
stay

THE MOTHER
Yes
Don't go

THE BOY
   I don't have to go
   just yet
   There's no rush
   There's nothing waiting

THE MOTHER
   No don't go
   Stay for a while
   Pause. Looks at him
   Everything's so horrible

THE BOY
   I won't carry on about it
   But

THE MOTHER
   Calmly
   I shouldn't have
   Short pause

THE BOY
   But it is a bit strange to think
   that if it hadn't been
   for that committee

THE MOTHER
   Yes
   But everything was so difficult
   back then
   I

THE BOY
   Well I'm sorry
   But
   As it's about my life
   in a way
   anyway
   I did want to know

THE MOTHER
Yes

THE BOY
It's embarrassing to talk about
I understand that
Why don't we

THE MOTHER
Yes
I don't know
Pause
But you
Short pause
I'll tell you something
You're a lot like me
Yes I know you didn't expect
to hear me say that
But actually

THE BOY
Why not

THE MOTHER
When I listen to you
it's like listening to myself
not what you're saying
Because you hardly say anything
Short laugh, wounded
not the way you look
But something else

THE BOY
Yes

THE MOTHER
There's something
Short pause. Searching for something to say
And I didn't visit my mother either
for many years

just like you
She laughs
Because we were always fighting
we always disagreed
Believed in completely different things
Well believed in
I don't believe in anything
any more
not now
But my mother

THE BOY
Goes and sits down
Tell me about you and your mother
then

THE MOTHER
No it was nothing

THE BOY
Come on

THE MOTHER
No

THE BOY
Come on tell me

THE MOTHER
Well what I was going to say about
me and my mother was
that well
That my mother and I
Near tears
were always fighting
and

THE BOY
Well she was
a devout Christian

as they say
your mother

THE MOTHER
Yes
you could say that

THE BOY
So you had fights

THE MOTHER
Yes we had fights

THE BOY
She believed in God
and you didn't believe in God

THE MOTHER
No
And I said the ugliest things
to her

THE BOY
Yes

THE MOTHER
I said
if heaven is what she would
like it to be
then I wouldn't want to go there
I said to her
I said things like that
To a woman who'd always supported the Mission
as she called it
she went to the Mission
all her life
and she had to listen to
me declaring myself a heathen
Short pause
I'm a heathen
I said to her

I'm a heathen
And do you know what she answered
No you're not a heathen
she said
She begins to laugh
Yes that's how it was

THE BOY
Yes she believed
in
Short pause
I don't know
what's best or worst
myself

THE MOTHER
No
me neither
Not anymore

THE BOY
But I don't know
Short pause. Gets up
I don't know
But she was good to me
my grandma
And then
Looks at his mother
she talked about Jesus
about Jesus
and about the angels
About God
She talked about Canaan's land

THE MOTHER
Yes she did
all the time

THE BOY
And it sounded so strange

I thought
Canaan's land

THE MOTHER
Yes

THE BOY
Canaan's land
He smiles
And she told me she prayed for me
At night
in her bed
she'd lie there
and think about me
and concentrate her power on a picture of me
I can see her lying there
concentrating her power on the picture she had
of me
the picture she had inside her head
and she turned that picture
towards something she knew was there
and that she called Jesus
called God
that she thought would help me
Knew would help me

THE MOTHER
Laughs
And wouldn't let people like me
go to the local dance parties
Not that that's too important
Play cards
Wear my hair loose
she wouldn't let me

THE BOY
I know
You've told me

THE MOTHER
To look at a man

not to mention dance with one
she wouldn't let me
She wouldn't let me
have a single thought that was mine
Yes I'm sure it was just as well
the way I look at it now
But

THE BOY
Perhaps

THE MOTHER
All she wanted me to do was recite prayers
Read Bible texts
and then
maybe
read Christian stories
about conversion
and joy
Oh what a great joy
And about life on the straight and narrow

THE BOY
Yes yes

THE MOTHER
Yes that's how it was

THE BOY
But now your mother's dead
My grandma's dead

THE MOTHER
Yes the woman who gave you more than anyone else
as you've said
Yes that's what you said
Yes
And I'm sure it's
true too
She has been more important to you

than I have
I know that
Pause. In despair
But
No I don't know
Why don't you say something to me
tell me something
Can't you tell me something
from Ireland
from Germany
Was it Dublin you went to
Tell me what you're doing in Oslo

THE BOY
My grandma
is the only one
who's been nothing but good
to me all my life
Yes
that's true
And those years I lived
with her and granddad
are the best years
of my whole life
Grandma was always good to me

THE MOTHER
Perhaps

THE BOY
She was

THE MOTHER
Yes
Short pause

THE BOY
Why do you always
say horrible things about her

THE MOTHER
Do I
really
I don't mean to

THE BOY
Perhaps you don't

THE MOTHER
Not that I'm aware of

THE BOY
Maybe you don't

THE MOTHER
I'm so tired
I don't know any more

THE BOY
Yes

THE MOTHER
So terribly tired

THE BOY
I suppose it wasn't easy for you
to be there at your mother's
funeral

THE MOTHER
It was
terrible

THE BOY
Yes

THE MOTHER
It was truly terrible
And that's where I saw your father again
too
I hadn't seen him
for many years
Everything seemed to conspire against me

> *She laughs*
> I haven't quite
> got over it
> yet
> When I think about it
> it still hurts

THE BOY
> Yes

THE MOTHER
> And if I'd known how it would be
> I wouldn't have turned up
> even if it was my own mother's funeral
> Yes I mean that
> I wouldn't have turned up

THE BOY
> Really
> *Pause*

THE MOTHER
> I couldn't have gone through it

THE BOY
> No

THE MOTHER
> But I'm sure she's in her heaven
> now
> your grandma

THE BOY
> You're not going there
> when you die

THE MOTHER
> How do I know

THE BOY
> Life is over
> when this life is over

Finished is finished
And so you rest
But what if that's not how it is

THE MOTHER
Yes
You're frightening me

THE BOY
There might be something else
something more

THE MOTHER
I'm not stupid

THE BOY
Somehow in some way
something more
Everyone knows that
anyway
And all the good literature
you don't read
knows that

THE MOTHER
Stop talking
nonsense
It sounds so stupid

THE BOY
Why not simply kill all the old people
I mean
instead of the unborn children

THE MOTHER
Well said
For instance your grandma

THE BOY
She's dead already
The old ones should be killed

and not the little unborn children
For there's nothing weaker
than an unborn child

THE MOTHER
Oh how beautifully put

THE BOY
But it's embarrassing
to stand here and say these things
You're right
I shouldn't do it
I'm defending myself
Why do I do that

THE MOTHER
Your father shouldn't have told you
Interrupts herself

THE BOY
So you don't think I shouldn't have known

THE MOTHER
You and your grandmother
My mother
I should've taken my own life
a long time ago
I can easily take my own life

THE BOY
Perhaps
Quickly
No I don't mean that

THE MOTHER
Do you mean it

THE BOY
I don't know
No I don't mean it

THE MOTHER

Of course you don't know
You know nothing
do you
nothing
You've studied abroad
sort of
at least for a bit
but most of your life
you've kept to yourself
on the West Coast
you and your father
and that woman
yes the one who puts up with so much
That's what
you have done
And you're chatting on
about Beckett and Joyce
and what's-their-names
You're just like your father
Keep bragging
I'm not sixteen
I'm not impressed by you
Don't waste your time
She starts laughing. Pause
Oh dear
Long pause
No I won't
Pause
But couldn't we
Short pause
We see each other so rarely
we're hardly ever
together
And we've had some good times
too
together

many times
right
You and I
Fishing
with my father
in his old rowboat
Hiking in the mountains
Fishing
right
We used to row out to the reef
We used to light a bonfire
there
Then
Yes
I care a lot about you
of course I do
But I was so young
So young and stupid
I was a believer in a way
in my own way
I was going to university
I was going to make something of myself
The timing was all wrong
to become a mother
It was all wrong
I thought
but then it wasn't really
so bad
after all
It turned out alright

THE BOY
But you left me with grandma
and then with my dad
when she became too frail
for me to live
with her

You just left
I'm not accusing you
even if it sounds like that
don't take it the wrong way
But

THE MOTHER
You're right
it's true
I shouldn't have
Yes and it was
well it was how it should be
It was right
because it was wrong
And you can understand that
can't you

THE BOY
Nods
Yes

THE MOTHER
You understand that

THE BOY
Maybe
And I've said
that you might as well have got rid of me
It would've been for the best
I mean that
But I
Laughs a little
don't suppose I warm to the thought
that I should've been thrown on
some rubbish heap

THE MOTHER
But that's not what happens
It's not like that

69

THE BOY
What happens

THE MOTHER
I'm not sure
But not that
in any case
It's not like that

THE BOY
No perhaps not
He takes out the packet of cigarettes, lights one. He holds out the packet to her, she takes a cigarette, he lights his lighter, holds it out to her, lights her cigarette too

THE MOTHER
I want to tell you
but you won't believe it
that I care more about you
than I care about myself
Short pause
I want you to know that
If it's a question of
your life or mine
they can just take mine

THE BOY
Don't say things like that
They're just words fuelled by emotions
It just becomes
sentimental

THE MOTHER
But that's what
it feels like
So I'm
sentimental
then

THE BOY
>*Laughs*
>Alright
>*Short pause*
>Perhaps I should go

THE MOTHER
>No stay
>Tell me something
>something about literature
>about philosophy
>whatever
>Or tell me what you like

THE BOY
>What I like

THE MOTHER
>Yes what you like
>What do you like to read

THE BOY
>I like literature
>art
>But it sounds
>so silly to say that

THE MOTHER
>No
>But you know
>what art is
>then
>since you like it
>I mean

THE BOY
>Yes
>I think maybe I do

THE MOTHER
>What is art
>then

THE BOY
> If you don't know that
> I can't tell
> you
> I suppose that's
> what art is
> right

THE MOTHER
> Yes that's right
> I don't suppose I understand art

THE BOY
> And you don't really think I do
> either
> That it's just something
> I want to impress
> you with
> *He laughs, a little wounded*

THE MOTHER
> *Quickly*
> I know I say things like that
> I say them
> *Looks at him*
> But I don't mean them
> Because I too

THE BOY
> Yes I suppose you understand art
> you too

THE MOTHER
> *Laughs*
> You and I
> are more alike than you think

THE BOY
> Yes you keep saying that
> But what does art mean to you

THE MOTHER
  Shall I tell you

THE BOY
  Yes do

THE MOTHER
  The Glass Menagerie

THE BOY
  A little surprised
  The Glass Menagerie

THE MOTHER
  Yes
  A little happier
  I've read it many times
  And I've seen it as often as I've been able to
  I've seen it many times

THE BOY
  Why do you like *The Glass Menagerie*
  so much

THE MOTHER
  I don't know
  Every time I see it
  I always feel like crying
  sentimental
  that I am
  She laughs

THE BOY
  I'm sure you do
  I like Tennessee Williams too
  I too like *The Glass Menagerie*
  The Mother starts limping the way Laura does, is about to
  quote something from the play
  No don't
  Stop it
  I can't stand it

THE MOTHER
A little puzzled
You can't stand it

THE BOY
No I can't stand it

THE MOTHER
Why can't you stand it

THE BOY
You're always putting on a performance
Always

THE MOTHER
A little wounded
I suppose I am

THE BOY
Suddenly
I think I'd like to go

THE MOTHER
No don't go
Can't we

THE BOY
Continues
share a bottle of wine
together

THE MOTHER
Is there something wrong
with that too

THE BOY
No
I'm just talking
just chatting away

THE MOTHER
> *Tries to play Amanda in* The Glass Menagerie, *says the lines from memory*
> And where was Moses when the lights went out
> Ha ha
> Do you know the answer to that
> Mr O'Connor
> *She laughs*

THE BOY
> *Reluctantly*
> No

THE MOTHER
> Come on
> Do you remember the answer
> *He nods*
> Say it then
> No it's not your line after all
> it's mine
> But I'd much rather be Laura
> and you can be Jim

THE BOY
> *Shakes his head*
> No

THE MOTHER
> *Limps the way Laura does*
> Oh come on
> Now you say to me that I
> look like an old-fashioned girl
> and that you like that
> That you like old-fashioned girls

THE BOY
> No I can't do it

THE MOTHER
> And I say to you that I remember you

75

that I remember how well you sang when we
were at high school
I say
Short pause
I remember what a beautiful voice you had
that's my line
And you say
When did you hear me sing
Say that

THE BOY
When did you hear me sing

THE MOTHER
No not that
why don't you say
What have you been doing since high school
Say that

THE BOY
What have you been doing since high school

THE MOTHER
As Laura, limps
Nothing much

THE BOY
No I can't do it

THE MOTHER
Yes
Can't you just

THE BOY
No I can't do it

THE MOTHER
Yes
Now you'll say that you can hear music
and I'll say that it comes
from a dance hall

across the street
and then we'll dance
I'll say that I can't dance
and you say you want to
teach me
Here
Take my hands
as if we're about to dance
a waltz
The Mother takes The Boy's hands in hers, he lets her do it
reluctantly
Say it
Say you can hear music
She drags him with her in a few dance steps

THE BOY

No
I don't want to
Tries to get The Mother to let go of his hands, she lets go, and
walks around limping

THE MOTHER

Alright
She stops limping
That's OK
The Boy walks towards the door
The Mother watches him
Where are you
No don't go
The Boy leaves
The Mother looks at the door
We were having such a good time
Dancing together
and everything
No don't go
Why don't you tell me something
Don't go
Tell me what you were doing in Oslo

JON FOSSE

THE BOY
Answers from the door
I came to visit you

The End.

SLEEP MY BABY SLEEP
(Sov du vesle barnet mitt)

Characters

THE FIRST PERSON
THE SECOND PERSON
THE THIRD PERSON

THE FIRST PERSON
    Where are we

THE SECOND PERSON
    I've no idea

THE FIRST PERSON
    You've got to know
    you've got to know something

THE SECOND PERSON
    I don't know
    I've no idea
    Short pause
    I suppose we are
    Breaks off

THE THIRD PERSON
    At a distance
    Me neither
    Pause
    I don't know where we are either
    Pause
    But does it matter
    Does it make a difference where we are

THE SECOND PERSON
    To the First Person
    But I

THE FIRST PERSON
    Interrupts him
    Yes you've been here before

THE THIRD PERSON
    I've been here before too
    I've always been here
    even when I wasn't here
    I was here
    This is my place
    you could say

THE FIRST PERSON
> *To the Second Person*
> You're sure you have been here before

THE THIRD PERSON
> *To himself*
> I've always been here

THE SECOND PERSON
> I'm a bit uncertain about it
> It feels familiar
> and at the same time totally strange
> It looks a bit like my children
> But at the same time there's nothing here
> here where we are
> here with you
> or whatever it is
> that looks like my children

THE THIRD PERSON
> Your children
> Your children
> you keep saying
> There is nothing here that's like your children
> surely

THE FIRST PERSON
> *To the Third Person*
> It's still alright to say it
> surely
> There's nothing wrong
> with saying it
> *Pause*

THE SECOND PERSON
> It occurred to me that it looked like my children
> Because
> well
> *Short pause*

Because you can't say it looks like something
Because it doesn't look like anything
So I should be able to say
that it looks like my children

THE THIRD PERSON
But just saying that it looks like children
Pause

THE FIRST PERSON
To the Third Person
What do you think it looks like

THE SECOND PERSON
Do we have to be here always

THE THIRD PERSON
Yes always

THE FIRST PERSON
We must always be here
To the Second Person
It looks like your children

THE THIRD PERSON
Nothing
This doesn't look like anything
so then
Short pause
well then it's wrong to say it looks like
something
Only
Breaks off

THE FIRST PERSON
You know it doesn't look like anything

THE THIRD PERSON
Of course I know

THE FIRST PERSON
So you know that

THE SECOND PERSON
> But I still think it looks like my children
> *Long pause*

THE THIRD PERSON
> Look, why don't you give it a rest
> I'm sick of listening to you
> There's no reason all of us
> well those of us who are here
> should want to hear about your children
> OK

THE FIRST PERSON
> Must you say things like that

THE SECOND PERSON
> OK I won't talk about my children anymore
> I just thought
> *Breaks off*

THE THIRD PERSON
> We must always be here

THE FIRST PERSON
> Look why don't you give it a rest
> really it's
> *Breaks off*

THE SECOND PERSON
> I have given it a rest
> I won't say a word about it ever again
> no mention of my children
> I'll just go away
> And I'll never come back again
> You won't have to listen to me talking about my
> children any more
> It's that simple

THE THIRD PERSON
> Alright go
> then

Why don't you go
Just go away
Why don't you leave at once
I'm so sick of listening to you talking
about your children
I can't stand it any more

THE SECOND PERSON
I've hardly talked about them
I only mentioned them
just now
just casually
offhand
I haven't talked about my children

THE FIRST PERSON
Can't we
Breaks off. Pause

THE SECOND PERSON
I want to go

THE THIRD PERSON
Go then
Pause

THE SECOND PERSON
But there are no doors here

THE THIRD PERSON
No doors
well

THE SECOND PERSON
No there are no doors here

THE THIRD PERSON
Why should there be doors here

THE FIRST PERSON
Well can you see a door

87

Is there a door here
I can't see a single door
I can't see a window either
I am just here
and you are here
And I don't know how long I have been here
It's
Breaks off

THE THIRD PERSON
That's just how it is
Long pause

THE FIRST PERSON
It can't be just how it is
Nothing is just how it is
It's impossible that it's just how it is
It makes me afraid
I don't understand it
Short pause
I don't understand how I got here
I didn't make my way here of my own free will
I just happen to be here
I simply arrived here
It just happened
just like that
I find myself here
for no reason
I'm just here
all of a sudden
I find myself
arriving here
I don't understand why
I'm simply here
what's the reason for my being here
I don't understand anything
I'm just here

THE THIRD PERSON
We're all just here

THE SECOND PERSON
And we're going to stay here
We're always going to be here

THE THIRD PERSON
Always does not exist
To be does not exist

THE FIRST PERSON
We are here that's all

THE OTHER PERSON
Yes
we are here that's all

THE THIRD PERSON
To be does not exist

THE SECOND PERSON
To the First Person
And no one knows why we're here
What we're doing here
How long we have to be here

THE FIRST PERSON
We have to be here forever

THE SECOND PERSON
And we have always been here

THE THIRD PERSON
Always been here
I suppose
Always does not exist

THE FIRST PERSON
But why does it look like
no matter what I talk about

the woman I love
The woman I love
more than myself
Laughs
Yes of course
The woman I love
more than anything
The woman who
is the only one I have cared about
Enthusiastic
It reminds me so much of her
She
She is here
Embraces the space with his arms
This is her
I am inside her in a way
this place
it's her
she and I are this place

THE THIRD PERSON
Interrupts
It's not a place

THE FIRST PERSON
Keeps talking
it's she and I who are this place
and the others
are just here
they don't concern me
they don't concern us

THE SECOND PERSON
That's how I feel too
Pause
I too am in my love
This place is my love as well
This is my love
This is where I have always longed to be

Short pause
And now I'm here
Now I am
in my love
it's that simple
I understand now

THE THIRD PERSON
You don't understand anything

THE SECOND PERSON
No one understands
anything

THE FIRST PERSON
There's nothing to understand

THE SECOND PERSON
Understand
is something very different

THE THIRD PERSON
Understand
understanding does not exist
here

THE SECOND PERSON
To the First Person
Are you afraid

THE FIRST PERSON
A little

THE SECOND PERSON
Me too

THE FIRST PERSON
But it doesn't hurt

THE SECOND PERSON
No

THE THIRD PERSON
    It passes
    the fear disappears
    so don't be afraid
    The fear goes away
    Don't be afraid
    You are safe
    Don't be afraid
    Pause
    It's a good place to be
    Looks at the others
    Do you feel that too
    Short pause
    It's good to be here
    We are where we should be
    We are in our happiness
    We are free
    We are no place

THE FIRST PERSON
    Yes we are here

THE SECOND PERSON
    But here is no place

THE THIRD PERSON
    This is no place

THE FIRST PERSON
    No

THE SECOND PERSON
    No place

THE FIRST PERSON
    Nothing

THE SECOND PERSON
    No place and nothing

THE FIRST PERSON
    That's not possible

THE SECOND PERSON
No that's not possible

THE FIRST PERSON
No place
is impossible
everywhere is some place
so this is some place

THE SECOND PERSON
Have we been here long

THE THIRD PERSON
Long and short
we have just arrived
and we have always been here
This is where we are

THE SECOND PERSON
But why are we talking

THE FIRST PERSON
We are not talking

THE THIRD PERSON
Puzzled
We are not talking

THE FIRST PERSON
It just seems like we are
We know everything before it is said
and we know nothing

THE THIRD PERSON
It's frightening

THE FIRST PERSON
It's frightening for us all

THE SECOND PERSON
But it doesn't matter

THE FIRST PERSON
No

THE THIRD PERSON
It doesn't matter
at all
everything is the same
and it doesn't matter
Everything's gone
and everything's close
Everything's with us
and nothing
Nothing
and everything
Everything and
nothing
Pause
All our loved ones are with us
And none of our loved ones are with us
we are now our loved ones
and our loved ones are now us

THE SECOND PERSON
We all understand that

THE THIRD PERSON
Everyone understands that
and no one
everyone understands everything
and nothing

THE FIRST PERSON
There's nothing more to understand

THE SECOND PERSON
All that is over

THE THIRD PERSON
Now we are love
Now we are where love is

and the big peace
None of you shall
say a word more
now everyone shall be quiet
no thinking
no talking
Now the thinking is over
Now the words are over
Now it's time for a love
that no one can comprehend

THE FIRST PERSON
But

THE SECOND PERSON
It's not possible

THE FIRST PERSON
Quickly
It looks so much like my children

THE SECOND PERSON
It looks so much like the woman I've always loved
the woman who is my love
It's her it looks like
It looks so much like her
It's her
I am
when I am here

THE FIRST PERSON
It is my children
The children I love
Long pause

THE THIRD PERSON
It is your children

THE SECOND PERSON
It is the woman I love
Even longer pause

95

JON FOSSE

THE THIRD PERSON
It's the woman you love

AFTERNOON
(Ettermiddag)

Characters

ERNA

GEORGE

OLD MAN

ASLE

ELISE

THE SISTER

The living room in an apartment

Erna stands lost in her own thoughts, and George stands at the window, looking out.

An Old Man enters, he has long grey hair, but is otherwise dressed in ordinary clothes and carries a worn brown leather briefcase, he puts the briefcase on the living room table, moves the armchairs a little, opens the briefcase and starts reading.

OLD MAN
    And they will never understand each other
    Because such is life
    If we had understood each other
    what then
    what would have happened then
    what would have placed its one image
    in front of us
    No we will never understand each other
    Someone will always see one thing
    while others will insist on something else
    That's how it has to be
    Night and day
    Right and wrong
    an endless game
    of victory and defeat
    He smiles
    Yes that's really how it has to be
    That's human life
    Life and death
    Night and day
    Light and darkness
    Friend and enemy
    Accord and discord
    And that's how it has to be
    Because imagine
    He moves forward
    imagine if we were to live forever
    What would have had any meaning then
    Nothing
    Everything would have been evident

Everything would have been just what it is
And nothing would have had any worth
Imagine the boredom that would descend on homes and
      mountains
He shakes his head
But still people complain about death
as if death was the worst
But what would it have been like
if death had not
been there
Stares into the air with resignation
Then life would not have been liveable
That's
certainly true
Nods
death that makes life liveable
Birth and death
Night and day
That which is and that which isn't
He sighs, stands looking down at his open briefcase, mumbles
Oh well
I believe you must fear death
As you must fear God
Stands pondering
Yes
yes I believe that
Because we must make room
for fear too
otherwise it will be too tight
both for life and for death
He closes his briefcase
I fear God
and I fear death
And I shall soon die
He hesitates, takes the briefcase and moves slowly forwards,
bows, turns and looks at George, nods, and George nods back
and then the Old Man walks out and George looks at Erna,

she holds her arm out towards him and George walks towards
her, takes her hand. Erna poses somewhat pretentiously, her
head at a tilt, and then she lets go of his hand and George
stands there looking down. Erna goes to the sofa and sits down

ERNA
Looks at George
Come and sit down
Pause. George remains standing
Oh well if you don't want to
Pause
That's fine
really

GEORGE
I grew up by the sea
Short pause
We should go and see the house one day
where I grew up

ERNA
Yes that's
Stops. Short pause
We've often talked about doing that
Ever since we moved in together

GEORGE
It's a nice house
Small
but nice
The last time I saw it
It needed a coat of paint
The putty around the windows was cracked
But it's nice
It lies nestled between some cliffs
on an island
And there's a small country road
And in earlier days
each winter someone would disappear

at sea
They'd set out
and never come back
Erna gets up, moves forwards a little and stops
They just disappeared
Set out
and never came home again
Erna looks at him absentmindedly
But it's nice there
quite nice
at least when the weather is good
in summer
like now
We should go there some time
Shouldn't we
George looks at Erna, she still stands lost in her own thoughts,
as if she is resting in her own self
Do you want to

ERNA
Absentmindedly
Yes
perhaps
Short pause
We've been talking about it for a long time
ever since we moved in together
that's how long we've been talking about it
She laughs briefly

GEORGE
Yes
He looks at Erna's face, she stands there with her mouth half
open

ERNA
Wants to change the subject
If you want to
then
yes we should do it

GEORGE
Yes why don't we
Let's do it
Let's go

ERNA
Yes let's
Pause

GEORGE
Listen

ERNA
Yes

GEORGE
I like your face

ERNA
You like my face
Pause

GEORGE
As if he finally gets to say something
And that's why I can't stand
that you're always trying to show it off

ERNA
Taken by surprise
Show it off

GEORGE
Yes

ERNA
What do you mean

GEORGE
I mean what I say
I can't stand it
At home
when it is just you and me

alone
well like now
just the two of us together
then I see your normal face
or most of the time I see your normal face
but as soon as we go out somewhere
it becomes formal
it becomes sort of beautiful

ERNA
Confused
Right
She tries her best to understand
You want me to be
well
She looks down

GEORGE
Interrupts her
All I want
is for you to stop
Stops
I can see straight through you
Short pause
No that's not right
Short pause
I don't believe in you
because I am not aware of your doubt

ERNA
But you used to didn't you

GEORGE
Oh yes
I did
Laughs briefly. Pause

ERNA
I understand what you mean
Pause

GEORGE

A little happier
I love you much more now
than I ever did
That's why I'm telling you
Looks straight at her
Yes
Emphasizing each word
It is too stupid
Pause

ERNA

It isn't stupid

GEORGE

Isn't it

ERNA

No
Pause

GEORGE

Alright say it
Why isn't it stupid

ERNA

No
why should I
*Pause. George screws up his lips, makes them wide, opens his
mouth a little*
Don't be so silly
I thought you really liked me
you know

GEORGE

I do like you
Pause

ERNA

I understand what you mean
George looks at her modestly

GEORGE
You do

ERNA
It's stupid
but not so stupid

GEORGE
That's true

ERNA
It just happens
Short pause

GEORGE
But it's
Stops

ERNA
That's just the way it is

GEORGE
But do you like it

ERNA
In a way
Laughs
Yes of course
Pause
You used to think
A little hurt
perhaps you don't any more
but you too used to think
that I was beautiful

GEORGE
Nods with childish sincerity
Yes

ERNA
Yes
and what

GEORGE
Yes I used to think that

ERNA
But now

GEORGE
Well I still think
that you're beautiful
But not like before
Because now I know your face
Short pause
But it's much more beautiful
when it doesn't try to be
so beautiful

ERNA
A little uncertainly
Maybe

GEORGE
A little desperate
You believe that you're
well beautiful
And in a way
you are
of course
He laughs briefly

ERNA
Is it important

GEORGE
Yes
Short pause
Let's not talk any more about it
Pause

ERNA
>No
>You always think
>that I'm going to run off with another man

GEORGE
>*A bit cheekily*
>Well
>what do I know

ERNA
>It's not my fault
>that he called

GEORGE
>*A little resigned*
>No
>*Short pause*
>I mean what I said

ERNA
>You just don't want other men
>to look at me
>to find me beautiful

GEORGE
>You could be right
>but

ERNA
>But
>what

GEORGE
>It's not that simple
>either
>*George starts walking up and down, he continues for some time without saying anything. Then he speaks as if Erna is not there*
>It was quiet there
>quiet

Looks down
at home in our house
and the wind was merciless
and so many never returned
from the sea
Year after year there was always someone
who never returned
Young
old
remained
in the sea
And then her
Stops, laughs briefly

ERNA

Not to feel left out when you go to the shops
for instance

GEORGE

Still talks as if she is not there
Be
the distant one
in the shops
And then the dead ones
all the dead ones out there
And she always thought she looked so lovely
And of course she did
It wasn't that
She could never stand like a normal
Erna looks towards him, beautiful in a formal way
person
She had to stand
in this sort of
elegant pose
Lift up her face
in this elegant way
Erna lifts her face in a somewhat demonstratively beautiful pose
you know

Oh yes she was beautiful
At least that's what she
wanted to be
and of course
she was incredibly beautiful
Everyone thought so
But it became
Stops. George stops, looks at Erna, then she looks at George

ERNA
Let's have a rest
Pause
Come here
Leave everything
as it is
It's not important
It doesn't mean anything
That's the way it is
and that's not
the way it is
It's not important
You and I
that's important
Short pause
Come here

GEORGE
Nods
Yes

ERNA
Laughs a little
Come
here
Erna goes to the sofa and sits down

GEORGE
Yes

ERNA

A little sad
And we'll visit your old house
where you grew up
quite soon
yes we will
George nods
Come on
Let's get some rest
George nods again. Erna lies on the sofa, spreads her legs, and George lies down between her legs, he rests his head against her chest, she puts both hands in his hair, strokes his hair Pause

GEORGE

I mean what I said
I have thought about it for a long time

ERNA

Yes I know
what you mean
Pause. Erna strokes and strokes his hair. Pause. George lifts his head and looks at Erna

GEORGE

Your face is nice now
Erna nods
Your face is normal now

ERNA

Yes
Short pause
Yours too

GEORGE

Mine too
The Old Man enters carrying some empty boxes, he puts them on the floor and while he is doing that George gets up and goes out into the hall and Erna gets up and goes over to the window where she stands looking out. The Old Man arranges the boxes, the doorbell rings and Erna goes into the hall and the Old Man

*wipes one hand across his eyes and face, stands and looks at
the boxes while Erna enters from the hall followed by Asle. The
Old Man goes out*

ERNA
Stops, turns to Asle
Imagine you just showing up
totally unexpected
It feels really weird

ASLE
I tried to call
but

ERNA
I've just got home
I have
well
I'm going to move
the phone's been disconnected

ASLE
I was just passing and
Stops. Short pause
But if it's not convenient

ERNA
Interrupt him
No that's fine

ASLE
Sure

ERNA
Yes
Pause
I can't get over it
you standing there
at the door
I'd never have imagined

And you
you've never been here before
no of course not

ASLE
No
Short pause

ERNA
And you
Laughs briefly
well as you can see
Points to the boxes
I'm about to move
Have had people inspecting the flat
two inspections
well we
well you see
Short pause
I thought
Stops

ASLE
You're moving

ERNA
Yes
Laughs briefly
yes we
Stops
yes he
he and I
we
well he moved out

ASLE
Yes you told me

ERNA

On the phone yes
well
well I forgot
and
well
since it was my flat
then
just for once
I did what I felt
like doing
so I
A little lighter
well someone's coming to look at the flat
some time this afternoon
she's been here before
she's looking at it for the second time
I was sure it was her who'd come back
you see

ASLE

But then
well it's not convenient then
that I'm here

ERNA

Oh yes
that's
fine
Pause
Listen
Pause
well why don't you sit down
as you can see
there aren't many places to sit
but
the sofa's still here

ASLE
>Perhaps I should come back
>later

ERNA
>No stay
>if you like

ASLE
>I just thought
>*Stops*

ERNA
>It's good to see you again
>*Short pause*
>Just a little
>unexpected
>*Pause*
>I'm feeling really
>well really confused
>sort of
>Because there you were
>it was you standing there

ASLE
>Yes
>*Short pause*

ERNA
>I think the woman who's coming to see
>the flat
>might want to buy it
>It looks like that
>At least she's pretty interested
>So I'll be moving soon

ASLE
>Yes
>*Pause*

ERNA
>   It's been quite a while
>   since last time we
>   I mean since we saw each other

ASLE
>   Yes
>   *Pause*

ERNA
>   So how
>   *Short pause*
>   well how are you
>   I do think about you you know

ASLE
>   Good thanks
>   *Pause*

ERNA
>   Same as always

ASLE
>   Yes
>   *Short pause*
>   I was just passing
>   and I thought that
>   well
>   that it would be nice to see you again
>   you know catch up

ERNA
>   Yes
>   But I'm sorry
>   it's pretty empty here
>   It used to be much nicer here
>   *Laughs briefly*

ASLE
>   Oh I think it's
>   quite nice

Short pause
So why do you want to move

ERNA
I just felt like it
I felt that a change
might do me good
I suppose
Looks at him
and now that he has moved
Short pause
I told you didn't I
Short pause
It can get like that
something just has to happen
you know
that's what it feels like
and then
well
you do something
then
for instance
you sell your flat
or whatever

ASLE
Yes
Long pause

ERNA
As for you
I have
well I do think about you
of course I think about you
now and then
Laughs briefly

ASLE
Yes
Short pause

and I think about you
Pause
But
look at me I just barged in
I shouldn't have done that
It's not a good time
And not good timing
either
Laughs briefly
You having an inspection and everything

ERNA
It's fine

ASLE
But perhaps I should leave
And then we could
if it's alright with you
meet later
tonight
perhaps
or something

ERNA
It's fine
It's just someone coming to look at the flat
After that we can go out
somewhere
if you want to
Short pause
It's a nice day
a nice afternoon

ASLE
Yes
Pause
So you haven't bought a new flat

ERNA
No
not yet
But I keep looking

ASLE
You're not moving from town

ERNA
No
I don't think so
or maybe
it might have been a good idea
but
I wouldn't know where to move
so
Laughs briefly

ASLE
You just want a change

ERNA
Yes
Long pause
well
why don't you sit down
I mean if you want to
She points to the sofa

ASLE
Thank you
He remains standing

ERNA
Can I get you something
A drink
a beer perhaps

ASLE
That'd be nice

But
listen

ERNA
Yes

ASLE
I've thought about you
lately
quite often

ERNA
Looks down
Yes

ASLE
Yes it
Stops

ERNA
I have thought about you
too

ASLE
You see I hadn't thought about you
for a long time
you'd nearly gone altogether
and then I started to
well to think about you
I'm not sure how to put it
Short pause
perhaps
I
Stops

ERNA
I get so
Stops

ASLE
Yes it
Stops

So I
Stops

ERNA
I'll get something to drink
then
shall I

ASLE
Thank you
*Erna goes to the kitchen and comes back with a bottle and two
glasses which she puts on the table, she hands Asle a glass and
they sit down next to each other and she pours for them both*

ERNA
It has been a long time

ASLE
Yes
Long pause
But listen

ERNA
Yes

ASLE
Well

ERNA
Yes

ASLE
No it's nothing

ERNA
You can say it
you know

ASLE
Well it's just that

ERNA
Say it

ASLE
Yesterday

ERNA
Say it

ASLE
I thought about you yesterday

ERNA
Yes

ASLE
I was lying in bed and couldn't sleep
and then I suddenly started to think about you

ERNA
Yes
Short pause
And it had been a long time since you
Hesitates
had been thinking about me

ASLE
Yes quite long
Pause

ERNA
It happens that I
think about you too
They drink
Perhaps I should show you the flat
She laughs a little
no it's not much to show
really
Why did I want to do that

ASLE
Seems like a good flat

ERNA
　　Yes
　　Pause

ASLE
　　But you want to move

ERNA
　　Well you've got to do something
　　I suppose
　　Pause

ASLE
　　Perhaps I should
　　well I don't know
　　Short pause
　　perhaps we can meet
　　later tonight
　　or something
　　I'm not disturbing you

ERNA
　　No
　　Pause

ASLE
　　When is she coming
　　the woman who's going to look at
　　the flat

ERNA
　　Some time this afternoon
　　Soon I'd say

ASLE
　　Perhaps I should leave then
　　*He gets up, stands on the floor while she remains seated, he
　　hesitates a little, looks at her*
　　What are you doing this summer

ERNA
　　I don't know

ASLE

> Do you have someone to be with
> to go away with
> or whatever

ERNA

> *Hesitates*
> No
> *She smiles at him*

ASLE

> You're going away somewhere

ERNA

> *Gets up, stands on the floor*
> I'll wait and see
> I haven't quite made up my mind
> *Long pause*

ASLE

> It was good to see you again

ERNA

> Why don't you stay
> a bit longer
> Finish your drink
> at least

ASLE

> Yes alright
> but
> *Pause*

ERNA

> So tell me
> what are you doing these days

ASLE

> I'm
> *Stops*

ERNA
  The usual I suppose

ASLE
  Yes

ERNA
  Same thing

ASLE
  Hesitates
  Yes

ERNA
  Same here
  well
  apart from
  this thing with the flat

ASLE
  And it's not a small thing
  to move

ERNA
  No
  it's big
  yes
  Long pause
  But it was good to see you again
  after all this time

ASLE
  Suddenly
  I have missed you
  As if regretting it
  well in a way
  at least

ERNA
  Looks down
  Yes

ASLE
>No not like that
>I mean
>*Stops*

ERNA
>No
>don't say it
>*Pause*

ASLE
>I shouldn't have said it
>*Pause*

ERNA
>Well
>but

ASLE
>That's how it is
>I have missed you
>quite
>often
>*Short pause. He looks at her*
>I shouldn't have said it
>but
>well
>I've meant to
>to call
>but it
>*Stops*
>It's not all that simple
>It's
>*Stops*
>I couldn't just call
>either

ERNA
>No

ASLE

> Because you know
> you were living with that
> well with that man of yours

ERNA

> Yes

ASLE

> I've often thought about you
> very often
> and now
> lately
> when I had
> *Stops*
> No I can't say it

ERNA

> Yes just say it

ASLE

> No I can't
> *Long pause*
> How long is it since we
> *Stops*

ERNA

> It's quite a while since
> *Short pause*
> but we hardly know each other
> we haven't met
> all that often

ASLE

> No

ERNA

> So we
> well we haven't talked
> very much

so
Stops

ASLE
No
But I've often thought about you

ERNA
Looks at him
Yes
Pause

ASLE
And I have missed you
She looks down

ERNA
Don't say that
I get so
Stops

ASLE
Looks down
I shouldn't have said it
They both look down, then look at each other
You haven't
well you haven't found a new boyfriend
Laughs briefly
or

ERNA
No

ASLE
You are alone

ERNA
I suppose I am
Short pause
I'm sort of
well

I think it suits me to be alone
or
well

ASLE
Doesn't it get lonely

ERNA
Yes
now and then

ASLE
But you still prefer it
do you

ERNA
Yes
I manage really well
on my own

ASLE
But in the evenings

ERNA
I'm getting embarrassed now
She walks around a bit. Long pause

ASLE
I'm sure she'll be here soon
that woman
the one who's coming to look at the flat

ERNA
Yes
but perhaps
she won't come
That happens quite often
someone says they'll come
and then they don't come

ASLE
>Lots of people say they'll come
>and then they don't come

ERNA
>Some people
>at least
>it's happened several times

ASLE
>Yes

ERNA
>But I'm sure she's coming
>*Pause*

ASLE
>But listen

ERNA
>Yes

ASLE
>No it's nothing

ERNA
>Tell me what you've been doing
>I mean since we last saw each other

ASLE
>Not a lot
>or maybe it is a lot

ERNA
>Tell me
>then

ASLE
>Well I
>*Hesitates*

ERNA
    Or I can tell you something

ASLE
    Yes why don't you

ERNA
    Yes
    Long pause

ASLE
    Nothing I guess

ERNA
    That didn't go all that
    well

ASLE
    But
    listen
    I've missed you
    suddenly you're just
    there in a way
    when I'm lying in bed at night
    I can
    suddenly
    without having thought about you
    feel that you are lying there
    close to me
    And you are calm
    And it feels good
    calm
    yes
    And I feel a kind of light
    warmth
    no it's not warmth
    really
    it's just something
    well something that's there
    and it warms me

in a way
and feels
well it feels
Stops
And it's always on the left side
You are inside my heart
in a way
I can feel that you are inside my heart
Short pause
And
Short pause
we don't really know each other
well we've met a couple of times
But you're just there
here inside my heart
And we are calm
totally calm
Do you feel like that too
Or is it just me
Stops

ERNA
Looks down
A little
perhaps

ASLE
It's not just something I imagine

ERNA
Laughs
Not totally
at least

ASLE
I've been wondering
well if you lie in bed and feel that you
are lying close to me

when I feel like that
Or
Is it just something I'm imagining
Do you think you could
you could tell me
Stops

ERNA
I don't know what to say
I
Stops

ASLE
It's not like that for you

ERNA
Well a bit

ASLE
Maybe that's how it is
we're lying there
at the same time
feeling like that

ERNA
Quite shy now
Maybe

ASLE
And I become so calm
when you are lying there close to me
then I become calm
Short pause
And a little vulnerable
or sad

ERNA
But

ASLE
>And then it's calm
almost like
water

ERNA
>Like
water

ASLE
>Yes
It's true
It feels a bit like that

ERNA
>*Cheekily*
Like the sea
perhaps

ASLE
>Yes like sitting and watching the sea
Perhaps
one night
one calm night
and you just sit there
and you feel calm
and small
and big
in a funny way
small like yourself
and big like the sea
Laughs a little
And then it's warm
a warmth
something warms you
Short pause
And then it's calm
And then
well is it like that for you too

ERNA
> *Shyly*
> A little

ASLE
> But isn't it strange

ERNA
> Yes
> And a little
> well not dangerous
> but a little
> *Stops*

ASLE
> That we can feel each other
> *Pause*
> It has to mean
> *Stops*

ERNA
> I can't
> *Stops*

ASLE
> Now and then
> well I think I know how you are
> if you are calm
> if you are troubled
> if you are happy
> or if you are miserable

ERNA
> Don't say that

ASLE
> But it's like that

ERNA
> Listen

ASLE
  Yes

ERNA
  Well
  yesterday
  did you think about me then
  did you lie close to me
  Asle nods
  I thought about you
  too
  yesterday
  For a long time
  I was lying there
  I could feel you lying close to me
  Asle nods. She smiles at him

ASLE
  And then
  Stops
  Can I hold your hand
  She holds out her hand to him and he takes it, they look at each other, smile shyly to each other. The doorbell rings

ERNA
  Lets go of his hand
  That must be her
  the woman who's coming to look at the flat

ASLE
  It must be
  Should I leave

ERNA
  No you can stay
  Erna goes into the hall and Asle sits in the sofa, he drinks his beer. Erna and George come in

GEORGE
  To Erna on the way in
  So you've got a visitor

ERNA
>Yes
>*Pause*

GEORGE
>*To Asle*
>You're thinking of buying a flat

ASLE
>Yes
>I'm thinking
>about it

GEORGE
>I see
>well
>*Short pause*
>Do you like the flat

ASLE
>Yes
>it's a nice
>flat

GEORGE
>You want to buy it

ASLE
>I'm thinking about it

GEORGE
>Well it's certainly
>a nice flat
>*Short pause. To Erna*
>We agreed that I should
>drop in
>that I should come and get the
>stereo
>we talked about that
>didn't we
>*Short pause*

ERNA
> *Points to a box or two*
> It's right there

GEORGE
> You've packed it

ERNA
> Yes

GEORGE
> Good
> Thank you
> *Pause.*
> *Looks at Erna*
> It's such a nice afternoon
> sunny and warm
> so perhaps
> well perhaps we could
> the way we used to
> go outside
> have a beer
> some place
> I've brought a couple of glasses
> It's really nice outside

ERNA
> I'm showing the flat to someone
> I told you

GEORGE
> I can see that
> *Pause*
> But afterwards perhaps
> or what do you say

ERNA
> No
> not today

GEORGE
Oh alright

ERNA
Tomorrow
perhaps

GEORGE
To Asle
So you're going to buy a flat

ASLE
Yes
perhaps

ERNA
To George
Do you want a beer

GEORGE
Yes
I wouldn't mind a beer
Erna goes to the kitchen and Asle stands up and takes a few steps
You like the flat

ASLE
Yes
it's good

GEORGE
Yes
it is
Pause

ASLE
Yes
Erna comes back with a bottle of beer and a glass she gives to George

GEORGE
>   *To Asle*
>   I could do with a cold beer
>   it's a hot day
>   isn't it
>   *He pours beer in his glass*
>   It's such a
>   nice afternoon
>   *To Erna*
>   Pity we can't go outside
>   right away
>   sit in the sun
>   with a glass of beer

ERNA
>   A woman is coming this afternoon

GEORGE
>   The one you mentioned

ERNA
>   Yes

GEORGE
>   But afterwards
>   let's go somwhere then
>   and have a beer or two

ERNA
>   *Looks at Asle*
>   But

GEORGE
>   What do you mean

ERNA
>   No it's just that I'm going
>   to show the flat
>   *Short pause*
>   And you were supposed to

GEORGE
> *Continues*
> get the stereo
> But that can wait
> there's no rush

ERNA
> No

GEORGE
> Could come and get it tomorrow
> So when you've finished
> *Stops*

ERNA
> I've got an inspection

GEORGE
> Yes but afterwards

ERNA
> Maybe

GEORGE
> But we agreed
> that I should come here and that we
> *Stops*

ERNA
> Well yes

GEORGE
> It'll take some time
> before
> *Stops.*
> *Looks at Asle*
> You see
> well
> in this heat
> *He laughs. Erna becomes embarrassed and looks down.*
> *To Erna*
> Do you know what time she's coming

ERNA

    Some time this afternoon

GEORGE

    Let's hope she'll be here soon
    To Asle
    So you don't want to buy the flat

ASLE

    Maybe

GEORGE

    You haven't made up your mind

ASLE

    Hesitates
    No
    Pause. Asle looks at Erna
    I think perhaps

GEORGE

    Interrupts
    No why don't you stay
    You should have a proper look at the flat
    now that you're here
    I mean
    Asle remains standing, looks at Erna, George goes to him, puts
    his hands on his shoulder.
    To Erna
    Could you get his glass
    Erna gets his glass from the table
    You see
    well I
    she and I
    you see we
    Stops
    we don't live together anymore
    to put it that way
    so she doesn't always like me

coming around
but
well she
Brief laugh
well
She's quite good
like that
Erna hands the glass to Asle and he takes it
So you're getting a
Stops.
To Asle
Cheers
then
George lifts his glass to Asle and Asle nods and lifts his glass to George. They drink. Pause
Or perhaps
you know
each other
from before
you two
I mean

ERNA
Stop it

GEORGE
So you two
know each other from before

ERNA
Oh stop it

GEORGE
You have
met each other before
as they say

ERNA
Yes
Short pause

and
well he dropped in

GEORGE
Continues
Yes to look at the flat
I can understand that
To Asle
So you're going to buy a flat
are you

ASLE
To Erna
Perhaps I
Stops

GEORGE
To Erna
Oh well
George takes Erna's hand, holding it lightly in a couple of fingers, she lets him hold it for a while, then she withdraws her hand.
To Asle
And you
who
are you

ASLE
Well who am I

GEORGE
Yes

ERNA
Interrupts
Stop it

GEORGE
Well you are

ERNA
>   *Interrupts*
>   Stop it
>   *Short pause*

GEORGE
>   We've known each other for a long time
>   she and I
>   Great girl
>   don't you think
>   beautiful
>   right
>   even when she tries to make herself beautiful
>   she's beautiful
>   isn't she

ERNA
>   Stop it

GEORGE
>   It's that day
>   today

ERNA
>   Stop it

GEORGE
>   *To Asle*
>   Right
>   She's beautiful right

ERNA
>   Stop it
>   I get so fed up with you
>   I want you to leave

GEORGE
>   Listen to her

ERNA
>   Just go away

GEORGE
> *Questioningly*
> You want me to go
> But I'm
> I am your best friend
> you've told me that
> often enough
> that even if we don't live together anymore
> I am your best friend
> You've often
> told me that
> and today
> well it's such a lovely afternoon and

ERNA
> *Interrupts him*
> Please leave

GEORGE
> She's not always
> like that
> but now and then
> she's like that

ERNA
> God

ASLE
> *To George, uncertainly*
> Perhaps I
> *Stops*

GEORGE
> *To Erna*
> He is
> a bit perplexed it seems
> your new
> your new boyfriend

ERNA
> He is not my boyfriend

GEORGE
We did agree
that I should come
to your place
today

ERNA
Not today

GEORGE
OK
George puts his arm around Erna's shoulder

ERNA
Let go
George lets his arm stay where it is

GEORGE
What's wrong with you

ERNA
Why don't you go

GEORGE
OK
The door bell rings

ERNA
Let go of me
fuck you
George lets go of her

GEORGE
There are many people who want to inspect the flat
Erna goes into the hall.
To Asle
That's for sure
Short pause
And you're going to buy a flat
It's quite good
this one

why don't you just buy
this one

ASLE
Yes
well

GEORGE
It's a good flat
I know it really well
lived here
for quite some time
She hasn't shown you around then

ASLE
No

GEORGE
I can show you
around

ASLE
Hesitates
Well

GEORGE
Come on
It won't take long
There are only two rooms
this living room
and the bedroom
and then there's a kitchen
George puts the bottle and the glass on the table and goes to
open the bedroom door, stops and looks at Asle
Come on
This is the bedroom
it's not very big
but quite
alright
quite

good for its purpose
Come on
then
Won't you have a look at the bedroom
No of course not
I can understand that
Anyway come here
I'll show it to you
Erna enters from the hall, followed by Elise and her Sister

ERNA
To Elise
This is the living room
The Sister stops at the doorway, stands there and looks down

ELISE
Well I've already
Stops

ERNA
And the bedroom is
well
you remember that
of course you do

ELISE
Yes
Turns to the Sister
You can come in
you know
The Sister goes to Elise, stands next to her, looks down.
To Erna, as if apologising a little
This is my sister
I thought she could come with me
Wanted to show the flat
to her
as well
Erna and the Sister shake hands. Pause

ERNA
> *To Elise*
> Perhaps
> you two
> would like to walk around
> on your own
> look at the flat take your time
> have a proper look

ELISE
> Yes
> that would be
> good

GEORGE
> *To Elise*
> You like the flat
> *The Sister becomes restless*

ELISE
> Yes
> it's a nice flat
> *Elise stands there as if she is not quite sure what to do*
> Well, it's a bit difficult

ERNA
> *Continues the thought*
> to walk around
> in an unfamiliar flat

ELISE
> Yes

GEORGE
> *To Elise*
> I can show you around
> if you like
> *The Sister smiles to herself*

ERNA
To George
Don't be silly
The Sister and Asle look at each other, then they look down

GEORGE
To Elise
You're going to buy a flat

ELISE
Yes I'm finally doing it
I
you see I've thought about it for a long time
but
I kept putting it off
didn't get around to it
but then
well I grew up just down the street
Looks at the Sister
We did
The Sister nods
And then I saw there was a flat for sale
right here
so I

GEORGE
You live here
in this street

ELISE
No not now
But I lived here for many years
And she
Looks at the Sister
well she lives
here still
I lived here too when I was little
but then I moved
and then

well
I like it here
so
Short pause
Are you here to inspect the flat too

GEORGE
No
I just
dropped in
to pick something up
But I think
Nods towards Asle
he is

ERNA
Goes to the bedroom door.
To Elise
I'll show you
Looks at the Sister
Oh and you too
if you want to
show you around

GEORGE
To Elise
It's a nice little bedroom

ERNA
Just
Stops

GEORGE
You'll like the bedroom
I'll show it to you
if you like

ERNA
Don't be silly

ELISE
That's fine by me
To Erna
I mean if he's so keen
to
Laughs briefly
It's fine by me
really

SISTER
To Elise
But

ELISE
A little surprised
Yes

SISTER
Well I
Stops

ELISE
A little surprised
Just say it

SISTER
Well I

ELISE
Yes

SISTER
I was just thinking
that
Stops

ELISE
That what

SISTER
Well that
Short pause

that
Short pause
that it's not really right
you know it's
it's wrong
sort of
because
Short pause
really you don't need to
not for my sake

ELISE

I don't understand what you're talking about
Looks around quickly, apologisingly
don't need to
what

SISTER

Not for my sake
I mean
if you see what I'm saying

ELISE

Not for your sake

SISTER

That's right
Pause

ELISE

It's a nice flat
isn't it

SISTER

Yes
but

ELISE

Don't you like it

SISTER

Yes it's very
nice
Short pause
It's just
well it's not really
necessary

GEORGE

To Elise
I'll show you the bedroom
then
OK

ELISE

Yes
why don't
you
*George and Elise go through the open bedroom door and close it
behind them*

ERNA

To the Sister
Perhaps you'd like to see
the kitchen

SISTER

Yes that'd be good
Short pause

ERNA

Just go through
there
Points to the kitchen door and the Sister hesitates
You can go through
The Sister remains where she is
You grew up in this street
The Sister nods
Well if you want to see
the kitchen

157

SISTER
  Yes

ELISE
  It's through there
  The Sister goes into the kitchen, closes the door behind her.
  Pause

ASLE
  Perhaps I
  Stops

ERNA
  No don't leave
  not now
  if it's
  Stops

ASLE
  You don't want me to leave
  I thought
  well that you and
  Stops

ERNA
  No
  it's not what
  you think
  Pause

ASLE
  But that man
  Stops. Short pause
  You and he
  Stops

ERNA
  Yes but
  Short pause
  don't go
  It's not what you think

They hear laughter from the bedroom and George and Elise
come out, leaving the door open behind them

GEORGE
   To Erna
   She liked the bedroom a lot
   didn't you

ELISE
   Trying not to laugh
   Yes very
   nice

ERNA
   And the kitchen
   Short pause
   Well your sister
   she's out there
   yes you liked the kitchen
   you said
   didn't you

ELISE
   It's small and cozy
   I remember it well
   I really like it

ERNA
   Me too
   perhaps what I like best about the whole flat

ELISE
   It's a good flat
   yes
   And the kitchen is very cozy

ERNA
   The flat's nice enough
   I think anyway

ELISE
  Small and nice

ERNA
  And then you'd like to live in this area

ELISE
  Yes
  I used to like it here
  and well
  this is where I grew up
  of course
  Short pause
  There's no one else who wants to buy the flat

ERNA
  No one's made an offer yet
  at least

ELISE
  Perhaps I can offer the reserve price
  at least

ERNA
  In that case it's straightforward
  I mean the reserve price
  Yes that should be fine
  Short pause
  or
  perhaps
  no that's alright
  Short pause
  Have you looked at many flats

ELISE
  No
  This is the first
  To Erna
  You're going to buy a new flat
  or

ERNA
    Yes I suppose

GEORGE
    To Erna
    So you've sold your flat

ERNA
    It looks like it

GEORGE
    Then you can come out
    for a while
    let's do that
    celebrate that you've sold your flat

ERNA
    No
    you can
    go

GEORGE
    Looks at Elise
    Or perhaps you feel like celebrating
    That you've bought a new flat
    I mean
    that you've as good as bought a new flat
    And it's such a nice warm afternoon
    so

ELISE
    Looks down, shyly
    Could be nice
    I suppose

GEORGE
    Yes let's do that
    Let's go somewhere
    and have a glass of beer
    in the sun

ELISE
> Yes
> we could

GEORGE
> *To Asle*
> You didn't get yourself a flat
> did you

ASLE
> No

GEORGE
> *To Elise*
> Shall we go
> then
> before the sun goes down
> *To Erna*
> I'll come and pick up the stereo tomorrow

ERNA
> That's fine

GEORGE
> *To Elise*
> Let's go
> then

ELISE
> Alright
> *Looks at Erna*
> We'll talk later

ERNA
> *Hesitates a little*
> I'll call you

GEORGE
> *To Erna*
> And I'll call you
> tomorrow

I'll come and get the stereo
then
George goes into the hall

ELISE
About to go
Oh
my sister

ERNA
Yes
she's in the kitchen

ELISE
Goes and opens the kitchen door and speaks
We're going now
The Sister enters
You like the kitchen

SISTER
Yes

ELISE
Very nice
isn't it

SISTER
Yes

ELISE
I think I'll buy this flat
The Sister smiles
Might as well

SISTER
Yes
nice
flat
Short pause
But as I said
not for my sake

well you don't need to
I mean
Stops

ELISE
You should see the bedroom

SISTER
Yes
Elise and the Sister go and look at the bedroom from the doorway

ELISE
Nice
isn't it

SISTER
Yes

ELISE
You like it

SISTER
Yes
it's nice
Short pause
But perhaps
well you shouldn't

ELISE
You don't like the flat

SISTER
No I don't mean
it's
just

ELISE
I really like it

SISTER
Yes

ELISE
> *To Erna*
> Well I'll call you

ERNA
> Good

ELISE
> See you
> then

ERNA
> Yes see you

SISTER
> *Almost inaudibly*
> See you
> *Elise and the Sister go into the hall and Asle and Erna remain where they are, they look down, then they look at each other.*
> *Long pause*

ERNA
> I suppose you'd like to leave
> too
> now

ASLE
> No
> why should I

ERNA
> I just thought
> well that you'd want to leave
> now that you
> *Stops*

ASLE
> No I'd like
> *Looks at her, Erna looks down*

ERNA
> I'm so tired of
> *Short pause*
> yes

ASLE
> Yes
> *Pause*
> But

ERNA
> Do you want to leave

ASLE
> Do you want me to leave

ERNA
> *Hesitates*
> No
> not
> exactly
> *Asle goes and sits in the sofa. Erna goes and sits next to him and he takes her hand and she lets him take her hand*
> I'm so sick and tired of everything

ASLE
> Yes
> *Short pause*
> But now
> well now
> *Stops*

ERNA
> Do you want to leave

ASLE
> I don't have to leave
> or
> we could
> I suppose
> we could

ERNA

    It won't work
    You don't know me

ASLE

    Yes I know you
    in a way
    at least
    Long pause

ERNA

    It's probably just as well
    that you don't know me

ASLE

    It's not what you think

ERNA

    I'm sure it's a good idea
    not to say it
    He removes his hand
    I just want to get away

ASLE

    Yes
    Short pause
    But you don't want
    well you and me to
    I'm there
    anyway
    we could
    whatever you want
    She does not answer and he gets up
    So
    I think I'll leave
    then
    might as well
    And I'm sorry
    I shouldn't have come here

And I shouldn't have said
well the things I said
But

ERNA

That's alright
Long pause

ASLE

Well if you want me to leave
of course I'll leave
Pause
But
I'm there
you know
Short pause. He goes toward the hall door
You're sure you want me to leave
She nods. He stands in the doorway

ERNA

No don't leave
*She gets up, walks out on the floor and he walks towards
her, embraces her and they cling to each other and then they
let each other go and stand there and hold hands and the Old
Man comes in, he moves the furniture around a little, he starts
to gather up the boxes, puts bottles and glasses in a box while
Erna and Asle walk into the hall, holding hands. The Old Man
lifts up the boxes and goes out and Elise enters from the hall,
followed by George. Elise stops and looks at George, who stands
straight up and down*

ELISE

So this is where I live
now
Short pause
It took its time
before I moved in
Of course this thing
well with my sister

It's really terrible
isn't it
Pause
But
I'm here now
That it should happen so fast
with her
So sudden

GEORGE
Yes

ELISE
It's
Stops

GEORGE
Let's not talk about it
not now

ELISE
No
Pause

GEORGE
It's nice here
nice place to live

ELISE
Laughs briefly
Well you should know
shouldn't you
They laugh briefly
I thought you were coming on the bus
I was waiting for the bus
Short pause
I thought you'd told me
to wait for you
at that bus stop
where we arranged

to meet
But then you just came walking
along the footpath

GEORGE
Yes
Laughs briefly
I came on the bus
But
well I caught an earlier bus

ELISE
Yes
Pause
But
Stands there fumbling
Yes
Short pause
It's good
that
oh
God I get so embarrassed
It's
Stops

GEORGE
Shyly
Yes
Yes it's a bit mad

ELISE
Yes pretty wild
that you
well that you used to live here
and that I bought the flat
and then
Stops

GEORGE
Quickly, laughs
Yes
Pause

ELISE
And that we should meet
for the first time
that day

GEORGE
Yes

ELISE
Shall we sit down
*Points to the sofa. George nods. They sit down, she sits at a
distance from him. Pause*

GEORGE
Nothing
turns out the way you think it will
Everything turns out differently

ELISE
Yes
Pause

GEORGE
Yes
Well
it was her flat

ELISE
And now it's mine

GEORGE
Yes
Looks at her
No
Hesitates
no I don't know

    really
    Pause

ELISE
    If only it hadn't been for
    well this thing with my sister

GEORGE
    It wasn't your fault
    Pause

ELISE
    Yes but still
    Pause
    It's barely
    well
    in a way
    nothing's
    fun anymore

GEORGE
    Don't say that
    Pause

ELISE
    Looks at him
    And you

GEORGE
    Yes

ELISE
    You

GEORGE
    This thing with your sister

ELISE
    Yes

GEORGE
    Don't think about it

ELISE
>That was one of the reasons

GEORGE
>That you wanted to live here
>To live close to your sister
>*Elise nods. Long pause*

ELISE
>But listen
>*Short pause*
>I
>well I
>I don't know if I can be with anyone
>Not now
>I can't do it

GEORGE
>*A little disappointed*
>Yes

ELISE
>Yes that's what I often think
>That I don't dare to
>Well at least not now
>*Short pause*
>But I don't want to be alone
>either
>I can't bear the thought
>that for the rest of my life
>I'm going to live alone
>You know
>*Laughs briefly*
>But perhaps I just can't be with anyone
>either
>*Despairing a little*
>I think that's how it is
>I think I'm unable to be with someone
>I think I have to live alone

I don't think I dare to be with someone
I would be
Laughs a little
so afraid that he
well that
he
Short pause
would leave me
or just die
suddenly
just be gone
just like my sister
Pause
It's so terrrible
He nods. Pause
I don't think I can be with someone
but then I can't be alone
either

GEORGE
But you want to
Stops
You

ELISE
Yes
Puts her hands over her face
Oh this is so embarrassing

GEORGE
And I've been thinking
Stops

ELISE
Yes

GEORGE
I've always
wanted to have well

children
Short pause
Why did I say that

ELISE
Me too
A little happier
When I was little
Short pause
you see
Confiding in him
my mother told me that I used to play with dolls
all the time
My favourite reading was
catalogues with children's clothes
Short pause
And now
Stops

GEORGE
Yes
Short pause
She was your only sister

ELISE
Yes

GEORGE
I'm sorry
I shouldn't have said that

ELISE
You
Well
if I didn't have
you know
my work to go to
I really don't know

GEORGE
    Yes
    The weekends are the worst

ELISE
    Yes
    When you have time off
    and time to
    Stops
    Looks at him
    But
    Pause
    Listen
    Pause
    Suddenly
    Listen
    I have
    Beat
    I've bought some food
    Short pause. Elise is about to get up, but remains sitting

GEORGE
    Continues her change of subject
    And I
    well I
    I've bought a little
    a little something for you
    Elise remains seated and George gets up and takes out a small
    wrapped box. Elise gets up, looks as if she wants to stop him

ELISE
    Oh no

GEORGE
    Just a little something

ELISE
    Laughs
    Yes

GEORGE

Just a small thing
I thought
well
Stops. George stands and fumbles with the parcel
Yes

ELISE

Quite shyly
But you shouldn't
Stops. Pause
You
I have
well
A little embarrassed
I've been
thinking about
this
this
you know
Laughs briefly
so
so I bought some food
and stuff

GEORGE

But

ELISE

Everything's in the kitchen ready
It'll almost be like a house warming party
because you've got to have that
a sort of
well a belated house warming party
just for you and me
Short pause
Shall I go and get the food

GEORGE

Not yet not for me

ELISE
    Aren't you hungry

GEORGE
    No
    not very

ELISE
    We can wait

GEORGE
    As I said
    I've got
    He stands there fumbling with the parcel

ELISE
    I'm getting embarrassed
    No you really shouldn't have
    thought about
    He hands her the parcel, she stands there holding it, fumbling
    with it. She looks at it feeling ashamed
    No this it too much
    Long pause

GEORGE
    A bit embarrassed
    Well I wanted to bring you
    something
    when
    Stops

ELISE
    Yes

GEORGE
    I bought

ELISE
    Stops him
    But it's too much

*Looks at him. Pause. She sits down in the sofa, she sits and
fumbles with the parcel. Pause*

GEORGE

Don't you want to open it
Pause

ELISE

Looks straight ahead
Yes
but it's
I can see it's
well too much
Stops. Long pause
And it'll never work
Stops

GEORGE

A bit sad
No

ELISE

Despairing a little
It'll never work
After all it just couldn't work
Can't you feel it
that it won't work

GEORGE

Has to say something
No but

ELISE

No
Holds the parcel towards him
I can't accept
Pause
I don't know
Everything's so strange
It's not right

    really
    everything becomes so
    Stops. Short pause
    We
    well we
    Stops. Short pause. She gets up, puts the parcel on the table,
    looks at him
    I'll get us some food

GEORGE
    I'll help you

ELISE
    No I'll do it
    Alright you can help
    Just go to the kitchen
    and
    I'll come

GEORGE
    Tries to joke
    The kitchen

ELISE
    Laughs
    Yes it's through there
    Points

GEORGE
    OK if that's what you want
    I'll
    George goes into the kitchen. Elise looks at the parcel, then she
    quickly opens it and takes out a gold ring with a large purple
    stone, she tries it on one finger after the other, takes it off and
    hides it in her hand. George enters with a plate of shrimps

ELISE
    Hope you like shrimps
    Short pause
    Because that's what I

Stops. Short pause
I really do hope
Short pause
you like shrimps
Because that's all I bought
I thought most people like shrimps

GEORGE
Shrimps
is fine
*George puts the shrimps on the table, goes into the kitchen
again, she looks at the ring, puts it off and on her fingers, hides
it in her hand again. George comes back with a bottle of wine*
And you've bought
a bottle of wine as well
He puts the bottle on the table

ELISE
Yes
George looks at her worriedly

GEORGE
Is something wrong
She shakes her head, puts the ring on the table
George sits on the sofa
I'm getting a bit hungry
aren't you

ELISE
I'm not all that hungry
but
She sits down next to him
Still I could eat something
*Pause. The door bell rings. George looks at Elise, she stands up.
Pause. The door bell rings again, and Elise goes into the hall
and comes back followed by Erna*

ERNA
To George
Oh hello

181

Short pause
So you're here

GEORGE
Yes hi

ERNA
To Elise, apologising a little
Well I've finally come to fetch those boxes
Elise nods to Erna
I'm really
sorry
You're about to eat
She approaches Elise, looks at her
Sorry

ELISE
Uncomfortably
Your things
well they're in the cupboard in the hall
yes
I'm sure you remember where
of course you do

ERNA
Where
Looks at Elise
I put them
yes

ELISE
Well I haven't moved them

ERNA
I'm really sorry
You should be able to
Short pause
well to eat in peace
without me coming
to

Short pause
I could leave
I could come back another time
I mean
at a better time
It's just that I remembered
And then we had the car
this afternoon
But
well
he
Short pause
yes he's
coming
just parking the car
you see
and then
Stops
I shouldn't have come

ELISE
No no
You can get your things
No problem
I'll come
with you

ERNA
Good
Erna goes into the hall

ELISE
I
Stops
I

GEORGE
Yes

ELISE
> *Picks up the ring from the table, passes it to George*
> *Low voice*
> I can't accept it
> It's too much
> well in a sense
> I can't accept a gift like that
> *Despairing a little*
> Can't you see
> I can't accept it

GEORGE
> *Puzzled*
> Don't you like it

ELISE
> *Desperate*
> That's not it
> I can't accept it
> It's not possible

GEORGE
> You don't like it

ELISE
> No that's not it
> It's just that I can't accept it
> *Short pause*
> I can't

GEORGE
> *A bit sad*
> No

ELISE
> I can't
> I
> *Stops. Pause*
> I don't think
> *Stops*

ERNA

Enters from the hall

OK

I'm ready now

Why doesn't he come

he was only going to park the car

and then

he was going to come

Short pause

At least I can carry the boxes out in the hallway

ELISE

Nods

Yes

Erna goes into the hall. Pause. George puts his arm around Elise's shoulder, but she moves away, he removes his arm. Elise puts the ring he has given her into one of his hands

I can't accept it

GEORGE

Wounded

No

Pause

Do you want me to go

ELISE

No

you don't have to

Elise goes into the hall. George puts the ring on the table. Steps are heard. George looks towards the door to the hall, Asle enters

ASLE

Hello there

Just wanted to see how you are

I'm here to fetch some boxes

as you know

obviously

George nods

So

GEORGE
Yes
Elise enters

ASLE
To Elise
So now you'll get rid of
those things

ELISE
Yes
*Elise goes to the sofa, sits down. Short pause. Elise is about
to get up, but then stays seated. Elise and George look at each
other, then they look down*

GEORGE
Well I suppose I should
Stops. He goes into the hall

ASLE
So you
keep in touch
do you
*Elise nods. Long pause. Erna enters from the hall, stands in
the door opening*

ERNA
To Asle
Time to go

ASLE
It's all ready

ERNA
To Elise
Finally you'll get rid of all my things
Short pause.
To Asle
OK let's go
then

ASLE
    Yes let's go

ERNA
    To Elise
    Well thanks for being so nice
    about the boxes
    Stops

ASLE
    Yes thanks a lot

ERNA
    Yes
    To Asle
    OK let's go then
    *Erna and Asle go into the hall and after a while the Old Man
    enters, he looks at Elise for a long time, goes to the table and
    takes the ring, goes to her and hands her the ring and she
    stretches her hand out and he puts the ring on her finger and
    then the Old Man takes the shrimps and the wine bottle and
    carries them to the kitchen, and while he does George enters
    from the hall, he stands and looks out of the window*

ELISE
    To George
    Come and sit down
    Pause. George remains where he is
    Alright if you don't want to
    Pause
    That's fine
    by me

GEORGE
    Listen

ELISE
    Yes

GEORGE
>Why
>don't we go visit
>the place I was born

ELISE
>Why not
>This summer perhaps

GEORGE
>We were supposed to do it last year
>too but
>well you don't like to travel

ELISE
>No I'd rather
>well I've never enjoyed travelling
>much

GEORGE
>But I'd really like to show you the place
>It's by the sea you know
>It's very nice there
>*Short pause*
>I think it's nice there
>And the house I grew up in
>it's still there

ELISE
>Yes we can go
>but
>*Stops. Short pause*
>OK why don't we go

GEORGE
>It's a nice house
>Small
>but nice
>And the last time I saw it
>it needed a coat of paint

The putty around the windows was cracked
The house was pretty rundown
I should do some work on it
paint it
put new putty around the windows

ELISE
Yes

GEORGE
And it's in
such a good spot
nestled between some cliffs
out there right by the sea
You look out on the sea
from the house

ELISE
Yes

GEORGE
And it is
very isolated
No neighbours
Elise gets up and walks out on the floor

ELISE
But it's a long way to travel

GEORGE
Yes
Pause

ELISE
But of course we can go

GEORGE
I don't think I really want to go
either
but I think about it
I think about going there

And we've talked about it
pretty often
we've talked about
going there
Elise looks at him absentmindedly
And it's nice there
quite nice
at least when the weather's good
in summer

ELISE
Wants to change the subject
Let's get something to eat

GEORGE
Yes let's
Short pause
But listen

ELISE
Well
I'm a bit hungry
Are you

GEORGE
A bit perhaps

ELISE
You're not hungry

GEORGE
I am
well I could always manage
a bite to eat
*George starts to walk back and forth, and Elise sits down on
the sofa again while George keeps walking for some time in
silence. When he speaks it is as if Elise is not there*
And it was so quiet there
the way I remember it
it was always quiet there

Looks down
at home in our house
and very windy
the wind blows and blows
because the house is at the sea
and many never returned
from the sea
Short pause

ELISE
Yes
Short pause
Come and sit down
here next to me
Pause
Come over here

GEORGE
Nods
Yes

ELISE
Come then
Sadly
We can go back to the old house
where you grew up
soon
we can go there soon
George nods
Come here
George nods again. Elise lies down on the sofa, spreads her legs, and George goes and lies in her lap, rests his head against her chest, she puts her hands on his head, strokes his hair
Pause

GEORGE
Looks at Elise
Listen

ELISE
> Yes

GEORGE
> I like your face
> *The Old Man enters carrying his briefcase and he and Elise*
> *look at each other, then the Old Man toddles around for a*
> *while, opens the briefcase and starts reading*

OLD MAN
> And so it continues
> *Short pause*
> from one day to the next
> from one thing to the following
> so it continues
> A hand
> Two hands
> A face
> Blood and always a new fear
> A cry
> A long cry
> *A birth-cry can be heard*
> as if they suddenly understood
> that such cries shall only be cried
> one single time
> Before an ageing
> and a big and cool calm
> Towards other spaces
> Other dreams
> Other days of the dizzying song's emotions
> Of the coming day's time
> An incomprehensible coming
> An incomprehensible disappearance
> A language no one understands
> and everyone understands
> A will and another time
> *Pause*
> Life is us

and just the same time
For it will come again
to you
to me
from the redeeming will
of the unknown
it will come
And then it will disappear again
It comes to us
It disappears from us
It is with us and takes hold of its openings
and then just disappears
This is what life is
It is us who always
and never shall disappear
Short pause
It is us
*The Old Man turns around, looks towards the door to the hall
and the Sister enters, they gently take each other's hands, then
he turns around and opens his arms, Elise looks at him, George
sits up, they get up, and Asle and Erna come in from the hall,
holding hands, they stop in front of the Old Man and he lowers
his arms, turns around, opens his arms wide again, before he
and The Sister once more hold hands and remain standing in
front of the others*

The End.

BEAUTIFUL
(Vakkert)

Characters

THE GIRL (SIV)

THE BOY

THE MAN (GEIR)

THE OTHER MAN (LEIF)

THE WOMAN (HILDE)

THE MOTHER

ACT ONE

In the middle of the day

An old boat shed with double doors in the short wall; along this wall on the left stands a dilapidated old bench, on the left and behind it lies an overturned rotten wooden dinghy and on the front right edge the inner part of a pier is visible. A young GIRL enters from the corner of the boat shed and goes onto the foreshore, she stops and looks back towards the corner, but no one comes, and she becomes a bit worried, goes back to the corner to look and then goes and sits on the bench, keeps looking out, a bit annoyed. A young BOY enters from the corner, stops, looks towards her

THE GIRL
> *As if angry*
> Don't be so stupid

THE BOY
> Were you scared

THE GIRL
> No

THE BOY
> Just a bit

THE GIRL
> I knew you were just messing around

THE BOY
> How did you know that

THE GIRL
> I just did

THE BOY
> You don't know me all that well

THE GIRL
>*Firmly*
>Yes

THE BOY
>You've only just met me

THE GIRL
>Still
>*He sits down next to her on the bench*

THE BOY
>*Looks at her, as if a bit angry*
>OK
>perhaps you do
>*Short pause*
>But how could you've known that I didn't
>just leave

THE GIRL
>You wouldn't

THE BOY
>No
>I wouldn't
>*Pause*
>It's good to see you back
>this summer

THE GIRL
>It's been a few years

THE BOY
>And we were just kids then

THE GIRL
>And now we've grown up

THE BOY
>Yes

THE GIRL
Almost grown up at least

THE BOY
I have

THE GIRL
Interrupts him
Oh yes
you're a grown-up
She gets up, walks a few steps towards the water

THE BOY
We could go for a walk
along the shore

THE GIRL
We could

THE BOY
Or we could sit here for a bit longer

THE GIRL
Looks at the boat shed
That's a good old boat shed
It looks a bit run down though
looks as if it's going to fall down
any minute

THE BOY
It won't fall down
it's been standing like that
for ages
Quite short pause
It just keeps standing there
It'll never fall down

THE GIRL
In the end all houses
fall down

201

THE BOY
  Not this one

THE GIRL
  Stop being so stupid

THE BOY
  I'm not being stupid

THE GIRL
  Wondering
  It won't fall down

THE BOY
  No not old boat sheds

THE GIRL
  Old boat sheds
  don't fall down

THE BOY
  No they just keep standing

THE GIRL
  But the tiles
  on the roof
  are heavy

THE BOY
  They're not bothered by the weight
  those old sheds

THE GIRL
  Don't be stupid

THE BOY
  I'm not stupid

THE GIRL
  It's a bit spooky

THE BOY
  No it isn't

THE GIRL
Firmly
Yes

THE BOY
Isn't

THE GIRL
Sshh
Did you hear something
Is someone there

THE BOY
I didn't hear anything

THE GIRL
Oh well then
Pause
But there was something
I could hear something
couldn't you
I think it came from inside the shed

THE BOY
Shakes his head
No
Pause

THE GIRL
Who owns the shed

THE BOY
Gets up
He's this weird guy
Hangs around
Lives with his mother
although he's old
There are a few types like him
here
in the village

THE GIRL
   Listen

THE BOY
   Yes

THE GIRL
   I'm leaving again
   before long
   Soon my summer holidays will be over
   It will be autumn and winter
   It will be dark and cold
   and you'll be here
   and I'll be
   in town
   where we live

THE BOY
   Don't talk about that

THE GIRL
   And I suppose it gets very dark
   here
   when it's autumn
   when the autumn storms grab
   the walls and the roofs
   and the trees
   and the water
   in the fjord

THE BOY
   Don't remind me

THE GIRL
   And in winter
   when the snow settles on the mountains
   and the fields
   and the roofs
   of the houses

THE BOY
        Yes
        and the roads are so icy
        it's dangerous to drive

THE GIRL
        And on the fjord
        the waves are crashing white
        And it's snowing
        across the fjord
        Short pause

THE BOY
        And over there
        in the earth over there by the church
        Points over the fjord
        lie a lot of people I've known
        And you know something

THE GIRL
        What

THE BOY
        Continues
        I often wonder
        how they are
        under all that mould
        beneath the earth
        Lying there in their white coffins
        Especially in winter
        I wonder about that
        How they are

THE GIRL
        You may well ask

THE BOY
        We are here
        up here
        up here where it's day
        where it's light

and there
down there under the black mould
there they lie
in their white linen
Looks at her
I know a lot of people
I do
who've gone there
My grandma
My grandpa
some of my friends
lie there now
down there
in the mould

THE GIRL

Don't talk about it
You frighten me
Don't you frighten yourself too

THE BOY

Yes I do a bit
Short pause
I wonder about this
I really do
lying in bed at night
what if I
this minute
right now
now
now
die
they'll have to put me in a coffin
and dig me a hole in the mould
out there by the church
that's
Breaks off

THE GIRL
>That's
>Were you going to say
>*A short laugh*
>that is too awful to think about

THE BOY
>Yes

THE GIRL
>Let's not
>think about it
>any more then
>*Pause*

THE BOY
>Let's go for a walk
>along the shore
>then
>since we

THE GIRL
>*Interrupts him*
>Yes, let's

THE BOY
>*Looks out over the fjord*
>The fjord is quite calm today
>but the waves
>there are always
>a few waves

THE GIRL
>But today the waves
>are steady and calm
>*Short pause. She looks out over the fjord*
>The waves are rolling so calmly
>*Almost a chant*
>calmly rolling against the shore
>the waves are rolling and rolling

the waves are rolling so calmly
against the shore

THE BOY
Yes
Looks at her a bit mischievously, tries his own chant
Yes just like our hearts are beating
the waves are rolling
steadily and calmly
rolling and rolling against the shore

THE GIRL
Yes they do don't they

THE BOY
The waves are rolling and rolling against the shore
Oh yes they do
Anyway let's go
He laughs

THE GIRL
Stares ahead of her
I wonder what I heard before
I just heard it again
She looks at him
It was something
Didn't you hear something
He shakes his head
I think there's someone
inside the boat shed
Can't you hear
He shakes his head
You can't hear anything
He shakes his head again

THE BOY
Looks at her
Yes now

THE GIRL
You heard something too

THE BOY
Someone's coming

THE GIRL
I can hear steps

THE BOY
Come let's go

THE GIRL
Questioningly
Along the shore

THE BOY
Questioningly
Yes

THE GIRL
Yes let's
They leave quickly towards the right and from the corner of the boat shed a Man enters, he walks around on the foreshore for a while, stops and stands still looking at the boat shed and one of the doors is opened cautiously, he's about to leave towards the right, but stops when the door opens completely and the Other Man enters, when he becomes aware that there's someone on the shore he turns to go inside again, but as he's already been seen it seems too late and he remains standing there looking down, then looking towards the Man who is still standing on the shore as before, he too stands there looking down, then they both look up, towards each other, and smile shyly at each other

THE MAN
Moves a little closer to the Other Man
Well it's been a long time
Yes hasn't it

THE OTHER MAN
Smiles at the Man
Yes it has
Pause

THE MAN
> Imagine meeting again
> here
> at the boat shed

THE OTHER MAN
> *Nervous and embarrassed*
> Yes it's been a long time
> *He looks down. The Man comes closer to the Other Man*

THE MAN
> *Looks up cautiously*
> Must be fifteen years
> at least
> *Short pause*
> Yes
> it's incredible how time flies

THE OTHER MAN
> *Quickly*
> You're home on holidays

THE MAN
> Oh yes
> you could say that
> With wife and daughter
> *Short pause*
> She's nearly grown-up
> my daughter
> hard to believe
> But I suppose you know
> *The Other Man nods. Pause*
> Yes it's been a long time
> a very long time

THE OTHER MAN
> Yes

THE MAN
>It's incredible how time flies
>*Pause.*
>*Asks, even if he knows the answer*
>But you live here
>still

THE OTHER MAN
>Yes I'm still here
>You know

THE MAN
>*Speaks as if he doesn't know*
>So you've lived here all this time
>*The Other Man nods*
>You've never lived
>anywhere else

THE OTHER MAN
>Well I was drafted to the army

THE MAN
>*A little questioningly, despite knowing the story*
>But you didn't last long
>*The Other Man nods*
>They didn't want you
>*The Other Man nods again, and the Man laughs briefly*
>They sent you back home

THE OTHER MAN
>Yes I suppose they did

THE MAN
>I'm sure it was just as well
>I
>*Breaks off. Short pause*
>And apart from that you've been here

THE OTHER MAN
>Yes

THE MAN
> *Knowing this answer as well*
> You didn't get yourself an education
> or something
> *The Other Man shakes his head*
> You work at the shipyard

THE OTHER MAN
> Yes
> I've been working there
> for many years

THE MAN
> But you do some fishing
> in summer
> at least

THE OTHER MAN
> Yes I do a bit of that

THE MAN
> Do you get any fish
> then

THE OTHER MAN
> Some

THE MAN
> *Questioningly*
> Salmon

THE OTHER MAN
> Now and then

THE MAN
> And trout

THE OTHER MAN
> There isn't any trout in the fjord
> this year

Short pause.
Tries to change the tone
But last year
I landed six trout in half an hour
I
Points with his arm along the fjord
threw the rod along the shoreline
Very strange
Looks with some enthusiasm at the Man
and then a soft rain started to fall
and the trout started to bite and bite
I'd hardly pulled one into the boat
before the next one was on the hook
One after the other
Looks at the Man, smiles
Oh yes it's true

THE MAN
Sure sure

THE OTHER MAN
And this went on
for half an hour perhaps
and then it stopped
Strange isn't it
Pause

THE MAN
Usually you throw the line
all summer
without a single bite

THE OTHER MAN
Yes usually
Pause. The Man goes to the bench and sits down and sits
looking out over the fjord and the Other Man walks around for
a while on the beach, and stands and looks down, kicks the toe
of his shoe softly on the sand

THE MAN
  Still it's a nice place isn't it

THE OTHER MAN
  Still looking down
  Yes
  Short pause

THE MAN
  Very nice place

THE OTHER MAN
  That's what they say
  anyway

THE MAN
  Don't you think it's nice here

THE OTHER MAN
  Yes
  I suppose it's nice

THE MAN
  But you're used to it of course
  You see it all the time
  It's not nice in the same way then
  is it

THE OTHER MAN
  No
  then it's just
  Rather short pause
  where you happen to live
  Short pause
  You don't really see the place
  That's the way it is when you live
  in a place

THE MAN
  A little questioningly
  The place sort of disappears

THE OTHER MAN
> *With a brief smile*
> Yes in a way

THE MAN
> It's just there
> taken for granted
> sort of

THE OTHER MAN
> That's the way it is
> when you live in a place
> *Long pause. The Man gets up, walks a little on the beach,*
> *turns and looks at the boat shed*

THE MAN
> *Looks at the Other Man who still stands and kicks his shoe on*
> *the sand*
> And the boat shed
> we spent a lot of time in there

THE OTHER MAN
> *Lightening up a bit*
> Yes we played in there a lot

THE MAN
> Almost every day

THE OTHER MAN
> That was fun

THE MAN
> We had a happy childhood
> as they say

THE OTHER MAN
> Yes

THE MAN
> All the things we got up to
> in that shed

THE OTHER MAN
A little more happy
Up there
in the loft
there's still a candle
in a bottle
Looks at the Man
and the bed we made
of fishing nets
a couple of old sacks
Do you remember
The Man nods

THE MAN
It's been there a long time
It's been there
for thirty years
at least I'd say
Pause

THE OTHER MAN
And now you're home on holidays

THE MAN
Yes I guess

THE OTHER MAN
Are you staying long

THE MAN
I became a teacher
would you believe
Music teacher you know

THE OTHER MAN
With long holidays

THE MAN
You can say that again

THE OTHER MAN
And you've got your wife with you

THE MAN
>*Nods*
>Oh yes
>*Short pause*
>And the daughter
>of course

THE OTHER MAN
>Of course

THE MAN
>But you're not married
>*The Other Man shakes his head. Pause. A little exasperated*
>A married man
>that's me
>and a father too

THE OTHER MAN
>You went off on your own

THE MAN
>Yes

THE OTHER MAN
>You don't come here very often

THE MAN
>No
>*Hesitates*
>hardly ever

THE OTHER MAN
>Why's that

THE MAN
>My wife doesn't really
>like it
>here

THE OTHER MAN
>I see

THE MAN
    That's how it is

THE OTHER MAN
    But you're staying for the summer

THE MAN
    Looks like it
    Short pause
    You see
    my wife got it into her head
    that this year
    we'd stay here all summer
    Don't ask me why

THE OTHER MAN
    I see

THE MAN
    She holds the reins
    you see
    Laughs briefly. Pause
    Despite knowing the answer
    You still live with your mother

THE OTHER MAN
    Yes
    Pause

THE MAN
    Gets up
    Perhaps we can go out on the fjord together
    throw out some nets
    perhaps

THE OTHER MAN
    Yes we must do that

THE MAN
    Points at the rotten dinghy
    But I'm sure you've got a better boat
    by now

than that wreck
That's the old boat
isn't it

THE OTHER MAN
Nods
Sure
Pause
You remember
the old boat

THE MAN
A little questioningly
Your old boat
The Other Man nods
We used to go out all the time in that boat
Of course I remember
Pause. The Man goes and sits down on the bench and the Other Man goes and sits down next to him. Pause.
Looks at the Other Man
It was good to see you again
have a chat
like the old days
When we were young
we were always together
Enthusiastically
Home from school
then you'd come to my place
or I'd come to your place
every day
for all those years
we'd do that
Short pause
And it's a bit strange
that we've never got together
the few times I've been back
I have to say
Short pause

But I suppose I've been inclined
to stay at home
I haven't gone out much
the few times
I've been here
Short pause
But I often think about
well what we used to do
in this place
in this village
how we used to play
the things we got up to

THE OTHER MAN
Yes we had a good time

THE MAN
Yes
A Woman enters from the corner of the boat shed, she sees the Man

THE WOMAN
So this is where you are
Short pause

THE MAN
To the Other Man
Well this is my wife
The Other Man nods, looks down

THE WOMAN
To the Man
I just thought I'd come down
and have a look at the boat shed
you've talked
so much about
And I find you sitting here
outside the shed
Just like the old days
She laughs a little

THE MAN
>Yes it's
>*Breaks off. The Other Man looks at the Woman, and looks*
>*down again*
>Well this is Leif
>my old friend from school
>*The Other Man gets up*
>We were together
>almost always

THE WOMAN
>*To the Other Man*
>I've heard
>all about it
>*The Woman and the Other Man shake hands*

THE MAN
>*To the Other Man*
>Well I've told her about you
>*Pause*
>You like it
>in this place

THE OTHER MAN
>Well I live here
>*The Woman walks along the shore, stands with her back*
>*towards the Man and the Other Man, looks out over the fjord,*
>*and the Other Man stands and looks down too. Long pause*

THE WOMAN
>*Turns around and looks at the Other Man who doesn't look up*
>It's very nice here

THE OTHER MAN
>*Looks up*
>Yes

THE WOMAN
>Really nice

THE OTHER MAN
Looks down
That's what they say

THE WOMAN
The fjord and the mountains
still snow on the mountains
And look at the snowdrift on the other side of the fjord
The snow is shining
almost white
over there

THE OTHER MAN
Looks down
Yes

THE WOMAN
Looks at the Other Man
But in winter
I don't suppose
it's much of a place

THE OTHER MAN
No
But in the summer you know

THE WOMAN
And I suppose the wind's harsh out on the fjord
in autumn

THE MAN
Looks up
Yes it's incredible
how high the waves can go
on the fjord
Short pause
To the Other Man
Remember that time we couldn't make it back
to the shore

THE WOMAN
Quickly, to the Other Man
You couldn't make it back to the shore

THE OTHER MAN
Looks down
No

THE WOMAN
To the Other Man
Is that true
Tell me about it

THE OTHER MAN
No we
Breaks off

THE WOMAN
Goes closer to the Other Man
Please
Tell me

THE MAN
We'd gone pretty far out
*Points towards the fjord, but the Woman stands and looks at
the Other Man*
and then
well
the waves were so rough
and the wind so strong
that we didn't manage
to row against the current
The Woman turns to the Man, and he looks at the Woman
It's true

THE WOMAN
To the Other Man
I suppose you were rowing
were you

THE MAN
>We were both rowing
>as hard as we could
>*Short pause. The Man gets up and places himself so the angle*
>*between the Woman, the Other Man and himself makes a kind*
>*of triangle. Pause*

THE WOMAN
>*To the Other Man*
>But you got
>safely to shore
>in the end

THE MAN
>*Looks at the Other Man, who still stands and looks down*
>In a way

THE OTHER MAN
>Yes
>in a way I suppose

THE MAN
>We were drifting further and further out on the fjord
>but pretty far out there's a headland
>jutting into the fjord
>and we managed
>with some hard work on the oars
>to get ashore there
>We pulled the boat up on the shore
>And went home
>on foot
>The next day
>when the fjord had calmed down
>we came back for the boat
>Didn't we
>*The Other Man nods*

THE WOMAN
>Didn't they get worried about you
>your parents

THE MAN
  Probably

THE WOMAN
  When they couldn't see the boat
  but could hear
  the strong wind

THE MAN
  To the Other Man
  I can't remember
  Perhaps they didn't know
  we were out on the fjord
  The Other Man shakes his head
  You can't remember
  either
  can you

THE OTHER MAN
  No
  *The Other Man goes to the bench and sits down, and the
  Woman follows him, sits down next to him, she sits there and
  looks out on the fjord*

THE WOMAN
  God it's a beautiful place

THE OTHER MAN
  Yes
  The Man walks over to the bench

THE MAN
  To the Woman
  Did you do the shopping

THE WOMAN
  Was I going to do the shopping

THE MAN
  No
  I was just asking

Short pause
And Siv

THE WOMAN
I don't know where she is
Pause.
To the Other Man
So this is the boat shed
you and Geir played in
when you were kids

THE OTHER MAN
Doesn't look at her
Yes

THE WOMAN
He's told me a lot about it
And you started a band together

THE OTHER MAN
Yes

THE MAN
To the Other Man
Do you still play
The Other Man shakes his head
Not at all

THE OTHER MAN
No

THE MAN
But you used to be so good

THE OTHER MAN
A bit shy, hesitates
No

THE MAN
Yes you were
Pause

THE WOMAN
What did you play

THE OTHER MAN
Guitar

THE MAN
And the violin
To the Woman
He was really good
on the violin
too

THE OTHER MAN
No I don't know
Pause

THE WOMAN
To the Other Man
Why don't you play the violin
for me
some time

THE MAN
And maybe we can come with you on the fjord
one night

THE OTHER MAN
Yes

THE WOMAN
That'd be good

THE OTHER MAN
No
I don't play any more
I've forgotten everything
He looks at the Man. Pause

THE MAN
You'll remember something

THE WOMAN
> *Gets up*
> Well I think I'll
> *Breaks off*
> *To the Man*
> Are you doing the shopping
> or am I

THE MAN
> I'll do it

THE WOMAN
> No that's alright
> I'll do it

THE MAN
> Alright then

THE WOMAN
> *To the Other Man*
> It was good to meet you
> *She walks around the corner of the boat shed and the Other Man gets up and stands in the doorway*

THE MAN
> *To the Other Man*
> See you then
> And let's go out on the fjord
> one night
> OK

THE OTHER MAN
> Yes
> We must
> do that

THE MAN
> Yes
> see you later
> then

The Man goes around the corner of the boat shed and the Other Man walks around a bit, then he sits down in the doorway before he suddenly gets up and enters the boat shed, and closes the doors behind him

Lights down

To black

ACT TWO

Towards evening

Both the doors to the boat shed are wide open and the Other Man sits in the doorway and stares out, then the Woman enters from the right, she goes out on the foreshore, stands still and looks at him and he looks at her

THE WOMAN
Questioningly
So there you are

THE OTHER MAN
Yes
Pause

THE WOMAN
Comes closer
Gently
So
this is the boat shed
I've heard
so much about
Pause

THE OTHER MAN
Yes

THE WOMAN
This is where you and Geir
were playing together
when you were little

THE OTHER MAN
Yes

THE WOMAN
But it's been a long time
now
since you've seen each other

THE OTHER MAN
Yes
it's been years

THE WOMAN
It's a nice old shed
Is it yours
He nods
Do you come here often
Here
to this shed

THE OTHER MAN
Hesitates
No
Pause

THE WOMAN
I thought I'd find you here
And I did
didn't I
He looks at her, nods
Short pause
Here you are
just as I thought
She laughs briefly
Do you sit here often

THE OTHER MAN
Now and then
Tries to explain, to give her a perspective
It's not really my shed
or ours
but we've had it
we've used it

for many years
so in a way
it's become ours
She stands in front of him

THE WOMAN
Looks around
It's a fine
old shed
To him
I love old buildings
Short pause

THE OTHER MAN
Yes
A brief smile

THE WOMAN
Listen
It's a great place that island

THE OTHER MAN
Yes
Pause.
Suddenly
You didn't tell Geir
I mean
you said
you wouldn't
tell him
because
Breaks off
I mean
Breaks off
Since you
Breaks off

THE WOMAN
No

A short laugh

THE OTHER MAN
Suddenly and unexpectedly
Once I said to this girl
that I'd give her a lot of money
if she undressed for me
or even just took off her jumper
I promised her
all the money I had
I was about twelve or thirteen
fourteen perhaps

THE WOMAN
Did she do it
He nods

THE OTHER MAN
I can't understand
how I found the courage
to ask her

THE WOMAN
But she did it

THE OTHER MAN
Yes
Pause

THE WOMAN
You've never been
with a woman
been someone's boyfriend
I mean
He shakes his head
Never

THE OTHER MAN
No
Pause

THE WOMAN
You come to the shed often

THE OTHER MAN
Not very often
sometimes

THE WOMAN
I see

THE OTHER MAN
Yes I come here
now and then

THE WOMAN
Why not
Pause
It's a fine evening
it'll be dark soon
and the fjord is nice and calm

THE OTHER MAN
I like it best
when there are a few waves
Pause

THE WOMAN
Feels she has to say something
And you and Geir spent a lot of time
here in the shed
when you were little

THE OTHER MAN
Yes
We had a sort of
secret room
up in the loft
There's a candle there
still
and a
well a sort of bed

that we made
of old fishing nets and things

THE WOMAN
Can we go up

THE OTHER MAN
No
I don't know

THE WOMAN
You're always saying that
I don't know
Short pause
But it was nice out there on the fjord
when you took me out in the boat
When we went ashore on the island
He looks at her, looks quickly down again
Were you and Geir always friends
when you were growing up

THE OTHER MAN
Well
not always

THE WOMAN
You had fights as well

THE OTHER MAN
Yes
Pause

THE WOMAN
You like to be on your own

THE OTHER MAN
I suppose

THE WOMAN
Don't you get lonely

THE OTHER MAN
>I guess I do
>now and then

THE WOMAN
>Can I sit next to you
>*He looks at her*
>Can I
>*She laughs a little and sits down in the doorway next to him.*
>*Pause. The Woman looks straight ahead*
>Well here we are
>then
>*Short pause*
>It's quite nice to sit here like this

THE OTHER MAN
>Yes

THE WOMAN
>Really nice
>*Pause*
>But don't you sometimes
>want to go away
>to experience something else
>something other than this
>I mean

THE OTHER MAN
>*Hesitates*
>No

THE WOMAN
>You don't dare

THE OTHER MAN
>Perhaps not
>*Pause. He gets up, goes out on the beach*

THE WOMAN
>Are you leaving
>*Gets up, goes over to him*

Can't we just stay here for a while
Go into the shed
Happily
You can show me the shed
tell me about all the things
in there

THE OTHER MAN
I don't know if I should
Breaks off

THE WOMAN
It was good to have a chat

THE OTHER MAN
Perhaps I should
Breaks off. She puts her arm around his waist, leans towards him, and he just stands there, straight as a rod

THE WOMAN
Looks up at him
You don't have to go
yet
Short pause
Tell me something instead

THE OTHER MAN
Hesitates
What do you mean

THE WOMAN
Just tell me
something
She takes her arm away

THE OTHER MAN
What do you want me
to tell you

THE WOMAN
Anything

THE OTHER MAN
    There's nothing to tell

THE WOMAN
    Yes there is

THE OTHER MAN
    No

THE WOMAN
    There's got to be
    something
    She takes his arm

THE OTHER MAN
    No

THE WOMAN
    Say something
    anything
    *He removes his arm from hers, but she grabs his hand, and she
    stands there holding his hand*
    Come let's go into the shed
    She pulls him with her towards the boat shed
    Why don't we go up to the loft
    yes let's do that

THE OTHER MAN
    Hesitates
    No
    He looks down. Pause

THE WOMAN
    What's wrong with you

THE OTHER MAN
    Embarrassed
    Nothing

THE WOMAN
    Laughs with surprise, a little afraid
    What do you mean

He removes his hand. Pause
Don't you want to hold my hand
She takes his hand back

THE OTHER MAN
I don't mind

THE WOMAN
But what's wrong with you

THE OTHER MAN
There's nothing wrong
with me
He removes his hand

THE WOMAN
Do you like me
He looks down
You're a funny one

THE OTHER MAN
Looks at her
I want to be alone

THE WOMAN
Starts laughing
Don't be stupid
We're not twelve
any more

THE OTHER MAN
I mean it

THE WOMAN
You want me to leave
He nods, then goes over to the bench and sits down
What's wrong with you
I think you've been alone
too much

THE OTHER MAN
Maybe

THE WOMAN
  Why do you want to be alone

THE OTHER MAN
  No I don't know

THE WOMAN
  Do people frighten you

THE OTHER MAN
  Hesitates
  No

THE WOMAN
  Laughs
  Oh don't be silly

THE OTHER MAN
  Looks at her
  Suddenly, unexpectedly
  Why don't you like Geir

THE WOMAN
  I like him
  He
  Breaks off

THE OTHER MAN
  I think he likes you

THE WOMAN
  Maybe
  Pause
  Why don't we go into the shed
  up to the loft
  I mean
  Oh come on
  please

THE OTHER MAN
  You go

THE WOMAN
No I want us to go together

THE OTHER MAN
I don't want to

THE WOMAN
Let's go into the boat shed at least

THE OTHER MAN
Hesitates
No

THE WOMAN
What do you want to do
then
Pause
Oh come on
let's do it
please

THE OTHER MAN
There's a ladder
in the far corner
You climb it
You can do that alone
can't you

THE WOMAN
Was that how you and Geir
did it
He nods
What did you do up there

THE OTHER MAN
We were just there

THE WOMAN
Often

THE OTHER MAN
Quite often

THE WOMAN
    And then you started to play together
    started a band together

THE OTHER MAN
    Yes
    Short pause

THE WOMAN
    But then you both stopped
    you stopped playing in this band
    of yours

THE OTHER MAN
    Hesitates
    Yes

THE WOMAN
    Why don't you talk about it

THE OTHER MAN
    It such a long time ago

THE WOMAN
    Did you have a fight

THE OTHER MAN
    No
    not really

THE WOMAN
    But it was you who didn't
    want to go on

THE OTHER MAN
    Yes
    I suppose it was

THE WOMAN
    Well that's what Geir
    says
    And now you never play any more

THE OTHER MAN
No

THE WOMAN
You're strange
you know

THE OTHER MAN
Looks at her
I think I've got to go

THE WOMAN
Can't you stay a little longer

THE OTHER MAN
I want to
Breaks off

THE WOMAN
All right go then
if that's
what you want
Pause

THE OTHER MAN
Looks at her, gets up
I'll show you the loft then

THE WOMAN
Hangs back
I suppose it's quite dark
up there

THE OTHER MAN
Yes we've got to have some light
He pulls out a lighter, lights it

THE WOMAN
You brought it
so we could go
up to the loft

THE OTHER MAN
>Maybe
>I did
>*He goes into the boat shed and she follows him, the double door*
>*closes behind them. After a while the Girl and the Boy enter*
>*from right*

THE GIRL
>*Excited*
>There's the boat shed

THE BOY
>Why are you so keen
>to come back to
>the boat shed
>It's just a shed

THE GIRL
>How should I know
>*Short pause*
>There's something about it
>I don't know

THE BOY
>Something about it

THE GIRL
>Yes that's right
>I like it
>and I don't like it
>Whatever it is

THE BOY
>It's just
>an old shed

THE GIRL
>Yes

THE BOY
>Old at least

THE GIRL
Laughs
What do you mean

THE BOY
Nothing

THE GIRL
You're strange

THE BOY
Am I
Short pause

THE GIRL
I wasn't knocking you

THE BOY
I know that

THE GIRL
What's in the shed

THE BOY
Just some old fishing gear
things like that
Just things you find in an old shed

THE GIRL
I've never been inside an old shed

THE BOY
No

THE GIRL
But they're nice old buildings

THE BOY
Yes
I guess
Short pause
Do you want to go inside

THE GIRL
>No
>*Hesitates*
>Is it alright
>Just to walk straight in

THE BOY
>Course it's alright

THE GIRL
>Are you sure
>about that

THE BOY
>Well the shed's just
>standing there

THE GIRL
>Let's just wait

THE BOY
>You haven't got the guts

THE GIRL
>No not really

THE BOY
>Why not

THE GIRL
>I don't know do I
>*Pause*
>It's sort of

THE BOY
>Yes

THE GIRL
>It's sort of
>well wet and wild and dangerous
>almost

THE BOY
> *Laughs*
> Oh come on stupid
> *She sits down on the bench and he sits down next to her, then*
> *she leans into him and he puts his arm around her shoulders*
> *and then they smile to each other and he hugs her close to him*

THE GIRL
> It's the boat shed's fault

THE BOY
> All down to the boat shed
> *Short pause*
> You know what

THE GIRL
> What

THE BOY
> I saw the guy who owns the boat shed
> out on the headland

THE GIRL
> The last time you were out in the boat

THE BOY
> Yes
> And he was with a woman

THE GIRL
> No
> *Short pause*
> Keep your voice down
> What if
> he's in there

THE BOY
> OK
> And she was

THE GIRL
  Tell me
  tell me

THE BOY
  No I can't

THE GIRL
  Yes you can

THE BOY
  They were in his boat

THE GIRL
  And then

THE BOY
  No I can't

THE GIRL
  Yes you can
  tell me

THE BOY
  Well
  they were in his boat

THE GIRL
  And then

THE BOY
  Then they went ashore on the island

THE GIRL
  And then

THE BOY
  Well then

THE GIRL
  Tell me

THE BOY
  No I don't want to

THE GIRL
Come on
tell me

THE BOY
No

THE GIRL
Oh just tell me
you idiot

THE BOY
No I don't want to

THE GIRL
OK
I'll shut my mouth then

THE BOY
Me too
*They sit there in silence and after a while one of the doors in
the boat shed opens and the Boy pulls his arm away quickly
and the Woman appears, she looks at the Girl and the Boy*

THE WOMAN
*Surprised, looks a bit embarrassed at the Girl, who is also a
bit embarrassed*
What are you doing here
The Girl laughs. The Woman walks onto the shore

THE GIRL
Fancy you coming out of the shed
Well who'd believe
that
Short pause
I was just saying
it'd be good to have a look
go and see what's inside
an old shed like that
She looks at the Boy
Why don't we

THE WOMAN
>Yes
>*Short pause*
>Well it's
>*Breaks off. Then the Other Man comes out of the boat shed too.*
>*The Girl and the Boy look at each other*

THE OTHER MAN
>*To the Woman*
>Well I think I'd better
>get
>going

THE WOMAN
>*To the Other Man, embarrassed*
>Thanks for showing me the boat shed

THE OTHER MAN
>*Remains still*
>Well
>*Pause*
>See you later
>then
>*The Other Man disappears around the corner of the boat shed*

THE WOMAN
>*To the Boy*
>And you

THE GIRL
>Oh him

THE WOMAN
>You are

THE GIRL
>Just someone I know

THE WOMAN
>You live here in the village

THE GIRL
Yes
he does

THE WOMAN
Nice to meet you

THE GIRL
Well

THE WOMAN
I'd better be off
then

THE GIRL
Nods
See you later

THE BOY
See you later
*The Woman disappears around the corner of the boat shed. The
Girl and the Boy look intensely at each other, then they smile
at each other*

THE GIRL
So that's how it is

THE BOY
That's how it is

THE GIRL
Laughs at the Boy
But fancy her being in the shed
with him
while we were sitting outside and
Breaks off

THE BOY
And with him
Pause

THE GIRL
What do you think they were doing

THE BOY
Hesitates
Well

THE GIRL
Oh I don't know
Pause
Anyway now you've met
my mother

THE BOY
Yep
Short pause
Straight up

THE GIRL
Laughs
Straight up
Pause
That was my mother
alright
Pause

THE BOY
Flippantly
Was it now

THE GIRL
And the guy who showed her around the shed
played in a band with my father
when they were growing up

THE BOY
So I've heard
She kisses him lightly on the cheek, then she gets up

THE GIRL
Takes a few steps on to the foreshore, turns around
Let's walk along the shore again

THE BOY
 It was her
 Breaks off

THE GIRL
 Yes

THE BOY
 No nothing

THE GIRL
 Who was with him
 out there on the island

THE BOY
 Well you said it
 He gets up

THE GIRL
 Laughs
 Stupid isn't it

THE BOY
 Straight up
 She laughs

THE GIRL
 It's their mess

THE GIRL / THE BOY
 Straight up
 Pause. She takes his hand and they exit right, hand in hand
 Lights down

 Blackout

ACT THREE

Evening.

A small garden with old garden furniture, a table, a bench, a few chairs, over to the left we glimpse the corner of an old white-painted house in Swiss style. The Boy stands and looks down towards the fjord and the Girl sits in one of the chairs.

THE GIRL
> *Looks at him*
> You like living here
> here in this village

THE BOY
> *Turns towards her*
> This is where I live
> I don't know what it's like
> to live somewhere else

THE GIRL
> There aren't many people here

THE BOY
> No
> *Short pause*
> We were only five kids in my class

THE GIRL
> And as soon as you'd finished school you started working
> in the ship yard

THE BOY
> Yes
> *Short pause*

THE GIRL
> And now you're on holidays

THE BOY
Yes

THE GIRL
Good thing I showed up
then
to give you some company

THE BOY
Straight up

THE GIRL
You don't want to go away
on holiday

THE BOY
I don't really like to travel

THE GIRL
Me neither
Short pause
It's usually
such a
hassle
Short pause
So you like it here

THE BOY
Yes

THE GIRL
Me too
She gets up and she and he stand together and look out on the fjord
The fjord is calm tonight

THE BOY
Like glass
Short pause
Look there's your mother

THE GIRL
   Where

THE BOY
   Points to the right
   Over there
   she's walking along the road

THE GIRL
   Then it's time to go
   She's so restless
   walks all the time

THE BOY
   I guess she's
   Breaks off

THE GIRL
   Laughs
   Yes I'm sure
   Short pause
   It's pretty embarrassing

THE BOY
   Yes

THE GIRL
   I'll never be like that

THE BOY
   Agreeing
   No
   The Man comes around the corner of the house, he's carrying a guitar

THE MAN
   Oh here you are
   The Girl and the Boy turn around

THE GIRL
   Yes

THE MAN
Haven't seen your mother have you

THE GIRL
I think she's
coming
I just saw her down on the road

THE MAN
Yes well she's out walking
all the time
A short laugh

THE GIRL
Looks quickly at the Boy
We thought we'd go for a walk
too

THE MAN
Right
He sits down in the chair on the left and starts to play, gently and melodiously

THE GIRL
Looks at the Man
We'll be off
then
They exit right and the Man sits bent over his guitar, playing, then the Woman enters from the right, he looks at her, but continues to play

THE MAN
While playing
So you've been for a walk

THE WOMAN
Yes
I've got to find
something to do

THE MAN

>But you were away for so long
>I was getting worried
>*Laughs uncertainly*

THE WOMAN

>No need to worry
>I was only walking along the road
>out to the church
>and then to the hotel
>then back to the church
>I walked down to the church
>I walked around looking at the graves
>I found your father's grave
>too
>*He nods*

THE MAN

>*While bent over his guitar playing*
>Did you meet someone

THE WOMAN

>Not a soul
>*Short pause*
>There are very few people here
>*Short pause*
>It must've been boring
>growing up in this place
>*He stops playing, but remains sitting with the guitar on his lap*

THE MAN

>There were more people here
>when I was a kid

THE WOMAN

>It wasn't boring then

THE MAN

>Not when I was growing up

THE WOMAN
But you moved

THE MAN
Yes
Short pause
I had to move
*Pause. She sits down on one of the chairs, to the right of him,
and he starts playing again. Pause*

THE WOMAN
Well there isn't much
to do
in this place
Short pause

THE MAN
Still playing
No
Short pause

THE WOMAN
Basically all you can do is
going for a walk
Quite short pause
And we're going to stay here
all summer
Short pause

THE MAN
Stops playing, looks at her
We can go home earlier
even if we'd planned to
Breaks off

THE WOMAN
Do you think it's better
to stay in the flat
with you sitting there strumming away
on that

guitar
of yours
He hits the strings
That was good
You should play that more often
She gets up
Oh I don't know
honestly
She walks towards the right

THE MAN
Are you going out again

THE WOMAN
Turns to him
I can't just
sit here and listen to you
strumming and strumming on that
stupid guitar

THE MAN
Where are you going

THE WOMAN
I walked down the road earlier
I suppose I'll walk up the road
this time
Not a lot of other places I can go
unless I walk straight up the mountain-side
of course
Short pause
Or straight into the fjord
She laughs

THE MAN
No
Short pause

THE WOMAN
Laughs
So I think I'll walk up the road this time
Short pause

Up the road
Down the road
Either
or
Short pause
And no matter where you look
you'll either see that eternal fjord
or those eternal mountains
behind you are the mountains
and on the other side of the fjord
are more mountains
Fjord and mountains
Fjord and mountains
always
fjord and mountains

THE MAN
When we arrived
you said it was lovely
here

THE WOMAN
Yes it's lovely
it's not that
But it gets so boring
No people
just these mountains
and the fjord

THE MAN
Yes
Short pause
You're bored
She nods
But we can go home

THE WOMAN
Walks closer to the Man
Home to the flat

With you just sitting there
with your guitar
strumming and strumming
A short laugh
That's not how I imagined you
when I watched you up on that stage
with your long hair
Your hair flowing
down your back

THE MAN
That's a long time ago
now
These days I can't even

THE WOMAN
Interrupts
No I couldn't sit at home alone
Siv and I sitting at home
while you were out playing
weekend after weekend

THE MAN
Laughs a little
I stopped doing that
ten years ago
at least

THE WOMAN
Knowing she is childish and stubborn
OK OK
Pause

THE MAN
OK then
There's got to be something we can do

THE WOMAN
If only you'd had a boat

THE MAN
    We had one when I was a kid
    before dad died

THE WOMAN
    Not much use now
    Short pause
    Where's that boat
    gone

THE MAN
    My mother sold it
    *Pause. The Woman moves forward a little, stands and looks
    out on the fjord*

THE WOMAN
    There's Siv
    and her friend
    They're walking down the road
    She has already
    found a friend
    here

THE MAN
    As he starts playing
    Yes
    she has

THE WOMAN
    Looks at him
    Your mother

THE MAN
    Bent over his guitar
    She's inside
    Pause

THE WOMAN
    Looks at the fjord again
    And there's your old friend
    walking up the road

he'll soon pass
Siv and her new friend
Pause.
Turns towards the Man
I met him by the way
your old friend I mean
in the shop
the other day

THE MAN
Still bent over the guitar
You've spoken to him then

THE WOMAN
A few words

THE MAN
Absent-minded
Right

THE WOMAN
Imagine your daughter
has found a friend
A decent young man too
She moves towards him
She's like her mother
goes for decent young
country boys
She moves closer
And this is where you grew up
Fjord and mountains
Fjord and mountains
Long pause
Fjord and mountains
and rain
Pause. He still sits bent over the guitar, focused on his playing
The mountains
And this narrow road
A few houses

And the church out there
The church yard
The old hotel
big
needs a new coat of paint
A few bus stops
A house here
A house there
Pause
What are you playing

THE MAN
Almost happy
Listen to this little tune
He looks at her, starts to play it again, she stands and listens,
then looks out on the fjord again

THE WOMAN
And there is
Siv walking
hand in hand
with this
boy of hers
A short laugh
Isn't she incredible
He doesn't look up, sits bent over the guitar with concentration
She's lucky
she has already found a friend
Did you know that
It didn't take long
He stops playing and she turns to him
That's a nice tune
Short pause
You're quite good
Short pause
But nothing happens
with all those songs
you keep writing

THE MAN
    That doesn't matter
    Pause. She turns towards the fjord again, and then turns back
    to him

THE WOMAN
    Don't you want to watch your daughter
    walk along the road
    hand in hand
    with a boy
    come on
    Come and look

THE MAN
    No
    She can do what she likes

THE WOMAN
    And you're saying that
    you
    her father

THE MAN
    Yes

THE WOMAN
    Well you're on holidays

THE MAN
    Yes

THE WOMAN
    And the rest of the time
    you're at your dull little school
    day in and day out
    teaching music
    and the odd subject
    besides

THE MAN
    Yes
    Pause

THE WOMAN
    Well
    I'll go for a walk
    then
    *He nods, starts playing again. His Mother, a woman of around
    seventy years of age, enters from the house, she nods towards the
    Woman and sits down on the bench, she sits and listens while
    the Man plays, he notices her, concentrates, finishes playing,
    and they smile at each other*

THE MOTHER
    It's so good to hear you play again
    And such a nice tune too
    Not like the sort of music you used to play
    To the Woman
    He'd sit
    yes it's true
    hour after hour
    strumming away
    Enough to drive you crazy
    Strumming and strumming
    It didn't sound like anything either
    Tried your patience it did
    Truth be known

THE WOMAN
    I believe you
    Pause

THE MOTHER
    And Siv

THE WOMAN
    Well she
    Breaks off. Short pause

THE MOTHER
    Who's to know
    where she goes
    Pause

If you're hungry
I'll make us some supper
We could eat out here

THE WOMAN
No thanks
I'm not hungry anyway

THE MAN
To the Mother
You already fed us
a big dinner

THE MOTHER
Still
The Woman walks around in the garden

THE WOMAN
To the Mother
I feel like going
for a walk

THE MOTHER
To the Man
If you want to go with her
that's fine by me
I'll stay here
just in case
I mean in case Siv
comes home
He looks at the Woman but she doesn't look at him

THE MAN
No I don't think so
not right now

THE WOMAN
I'll go
then
alright
She exits right. Pause. He puts the guitar on the table

THE MOTHER
You're clever on that guitar

THE MAN
I don't know

THE MOTHER
Do you perform now and then

THE MAN
From time to time
At the school where I teach
you know
But not very often

THE MOTHER
Doesn't your wife
Hilde I mean
like it here

THE MAN
She does

THE MOTHER
She seems
Breaks off
Well I don't
know

THE MAN
That's just how she is

THE MOTHER
She seems a bit
restless

THE MAN
Yes

THE MOTHER
Is something worrying her
Lowers her voice

She's not pregnant
is she

THE MAN
No

THE MOTHER
It's probably nothing

THE MAN
Not that I know of

THE MOTHER
Knows it's none of her business
Is she often like that

THE MAN
It varies
It's nothing

THE MOTHER
No I won't ask
Short pause
But you've certainly got yourself
a lovely daughter
At least she
likes it here

THE MAN
Yes

THE MOTHER
I can see that she's happy here
Pause

THE MAN
Yes
Pause

THE MOTHER
Puts her hand on his knee
It was really good to hear you play

like the old days
You and that guitar
She takes her hand away
You were always playing
in the morning before you went to school
and in the afternoon
the first thing you did
when you came from school
was to go straight to the guitar
and you'd sit and practice
hour after hour
practising

THE MAN

Well it wasn't
for the lack of trying

THE MOTHER

You can say that again
Pause
Leif didn't make anything
of himself

THE MAN

I think he just walked past down the road

THE MOTHER

Oh did he
I hardly set eyes on him
these days
he seems to like it best at home
hardly ever leaves the house

THE MAN

He told me he worked
in the ship yard

THE MOTHER

Yes he used to work there

THE MAN
   But not these days

THE MOTHER
   Shakes her head
   It's a long time ago
   now
   several years
   ago

THE MAN
   What's wrong with him

THE MOTHER
   I don't know

THE MAN
   Isn't he well

THE MOTHER
   I don't know

THE MAN
   How does he live

THE MOTHER
   I don't know much
   about him
   Short pause
   But his mother's on the pension
   They probably live off that
   Perhaps he's on a pension too
   he could be

THE MAN
   He doesn't play then

THE MOTHER
   I think he plays now and then
   with a teacher
   he plays the guitar

the teacher plays the accordion
They perform at weddings
and things like that

THE MAN
But not very often

THE MOTHER
No
once in a blue moon
The last time I spoke to her
to his mother
she said he didn't want to perform any more
He got too nervous
every time
she said
so he didn't want to do it any more

THE MAN
Oh
Pause

THE MOTHER
Moves into forbidden territory
Listen what happened
with your band
You broke up very suddenly

THE MAN
Yes
Short pause
Well it's hard to say

THE MOTHER
That's just how it turned out

THE MAN
Yes

THE MOTHER
>And then you lost touch with each other
>as time went by

THE MAN
>As it turned out

THE MOTHER
>Yes
>That's how it turns out

THE MAN
>Yes

THE MOTHER
>I feel sorry for him

THE MAN
>Yes

THE MOTHER
>Funny that
>he just stopped
>Lost heart
>sort of
>And he
>who used to be so full of life
>when he was a kid
>always on the go full of energy
>And then
>when he's around fourteen fifteen
>something happens to him
>It's as if he gives up
>in a funny way
>No one can figure it out

THE MAN
>No
>*Short pause*
>Does he go away now and then

THE MOTHER
>No hardly ever
>Not at all I don't think
>he stays here
>keeps to himself
>does a bit of fishing
>and the rest of the time he sits at home
>yes that's about it
>*Short pause*
>He's lost all incentive
>you could say
>*Short pause*
>And I did hear

THE MAN
>Yes

THE MOTHER
>*Continues*
>well that he'd been admitted

THE MAN
>He's been sick

THE MOTHER
>He lost his grip
>is what I heard

THE MAN
>He's not the only one around here who

THE MOTHER
>*Interrupts*
>I think it's the nature here
>It's too heavy

THE MAN
>Yes
>*Pause*
>It was awful when Dad

THE MOTHER
　But he didn't take long
　to recover

THE MAN
　And afterwards he was fine

THE MOTHER
　Yes
　That turned out
　well
　Short pause
　It hasn't always
　been easy
　Short pause
　I feel sorry
　for Leif
　Looks at him
　But I suppose it's
　not much anyone can do

THE MAN
　No

THE MOTHER
　And the years pass
　for him
　as they do for us all
　Short pause
　His mother's getting on of course
　It won't be easy for him
　to be all alone in the world

THE MAN
　No
　The Woman enters from the right

THE WOMAN
　So you're still here
　talking

THE MOTHER
> *Gets up*
> Yes
> so we are

THE WOMAN
> *To the Man*
> I turned around
> again

THE MAN
> Yes

THE WOMAN
> *To the Mother*
> I'm a bit sick of
> *Breaks off*

THE MOTHER
> Perhaps I should
> have gone for a walk
> too
> It's a lovely evening

THE MAN
> Yes

THE MOTHER
> I don't get out
> too often

THE WOMAN
> No I suppose not
> *To the Man*
> That friend of yours
> is standing down there
> on the road

THE MAN
> *A little surprised*
> Is he

THE MOTHER
Looks towards the fjord
Yes there he is
Leif is down there on the road
To the Man, almost happy
Why don't you go down and ask him to come up here
It'd be so nice
like the old days
He's just standing there on the road
Oh he looked up here I think
Why don't you go and ask him up

THE MAN
Explains, to the Mother
We ran into him
down at the boat shed

THE MOTHER
To the Man
Now you go down to him
and ask him to come up here
He gets up

THE MAN
Yes I'll do that

THE MOTHER
You do that
The Man exits right.
To the Woman
They were always together
those two when they were kids

THE WOMAN
Yes

THE MOTHER
Every single day

THE WOMAN
    I've heard all about it

THE MOTHER
    Nearly every single day
    But now
    well
    Breaks off
    I tell you
    I can't even remember
    when he was here last

THE WOMAN
    No
    Short pause
    And Siv
    she's not home yet

THE MOTHER
    I haven't seen her
    Pause. The Man enters from right, followed by the Other Man.
    To the Other Man
    Well well it's good
    to see you here
    again

THE OTHER MAN
    Looks down
    Yes

THE MOTHER
    I can't remember
    when you were here last

THE OTHER MAN
    Shy
    No it's a long time ago

THE MOTHER
    Yes it's been a long time

THE MAN
> *A bit happy*
> Not like
> when we were kids

THE MOTHER
> *To the Other Man*
> Then you were here
> nearly every single day
> *The Other Man sees the guitar*

THE MAN
> I've brought the guitar
> as you can see
> *Short pause*
> It'd be great to hear you play again

THE OTHER MAN
> *Looks down*
> I've forgotten
> most of it

THE MAN
> Oh it'll come back to you
> some of it will

THE OTHER MAN
> Not much there any more

THE MOTHER
> *To the Other Man*
> Is your mother at home

THE OTHER MAN
> I think so

THE MOTHER
> Perhaps I should
> drop in and see her
> so you young people
> can have the place
> to yourselves

THE WOMAN
Young and young

THE OTHER MAN
That'd be nice
She'd be happy to see you

THE MOTHER
Us old people
can have a bit of a
gossip
like the old days
Short pause
Yes that's what I'll do
To the Other Man
I've got to tell you
when Geir sat and played the guitar
just then
well it was just like
the old days
I could see him the way he was
as a kid
and then you've come here again
Well
She laughs
It's as if we've set the clock back
twenty or thirty years
I almost feel
a bit funny you know
She laughs. Short pause
Well you enjoy yourselves
And perhaps you could
She looks at the Man

THE MAN
Yes

THE MOTHER
You know find something to offer people
There should be something
Well you know where to look

THE MAN
Yes that's fine

THE MOTHER
I'm sure you haven't forgotten
She laughs.
To the Other Man
Nothing much has changed here
since you were a kid
The Mother exits right. Pause

THE WOMAN
To the Other Man
Why don't you sit down

THE OTHER MAN
Nods modestly, looks straight ahead
Yes

THE MAN
To the Other Man
I'm glad
you could come up
and see us
Pause
You should meet our daughter too
Perhaps she'll be home soon

THE WOMAN
Quickly
I'm sure she'll be home soon

THE MAN
Yes
Pause

THE OTHER MAN
Looks at the guitar
To the Man
You still play the guitar
then

THE MAN
Yes
Short pause
Don't you

THE OTHER MAN
I've stopped playing
I don't listen to music
either

THE MAN
I play a little

THE WOMAN
He plays nearly every day

THE MAN
Yes I suppose I do

THE WOMAN
Let's hope Siv comes home soon
She sits down in a chair on the right and the Man picks up the
guitar, sits down in the chair on the left, starts to play a tune.
Pause
To the Other Man
So you play the guitar too

THE OTHER MAN
I used to
I don't play so much
these days

THE WOMAN
You've stopped

THE OTHER MAN
Yes

THE WOMAN
Just as well perhaps
Pause
You don't have anyone to play with

THE OTHER MAN
Hesitates
No
Pause. The Man stops playing, puts the guitar down on the table. Pause

THE MAN
To the Other Man
So you still live here
then

THE OTHER MAN
Yes
Short pause
I'm still here as it happens

THE MAN
And in summer you go fishing

THE OTHER MAN
I do a bit of fishing

THE MAN
Perhaps we can come
with you out on the fjord
sometime
Looks at the Woman
That would be nice
Right
She nods

THE OTHER MAN
Yes

THE MAN
>   We don't have a boat any more
>   My mother sold it you see
>   when my father died
>   *Laughs a little*
>   *To the Woman*
>   You want to go out on the fjord
>   don't you
>   *She doesn't answer*
>   *To the Other Man*
>   Yes let's do that
>   *To the Other Man*
>   Do you want a drink

THE OTHER MAN
>   That'd be nice
>   thanks
>   *The Man gets up, goes around the corner of the house. Long*
>   *pause. Looks at the Woman*
>   I think perhaps I
>   *Breaks off*

THE WOMAN
>   Why don't you sit down
>   *The Other Man sits down on the bench. Pause*
>   So you don't play any more

THE OTHER MAN
>   No

THE WOMAN
>   Why not

THE OTHER MAN
>   I don't know

THE WOMAN
>   You don't like it

THE OTHER MAN
>No
>*Short pause*
>I think perhaps I

THE WOMAN
>Yes

THE OTHER MAN
>Well that I

THE WOMAN
>Yes

THE OTHER MAN
>That I should be getting home

THE WOMAN
>*Laughs*
>Oh come on
>*Long pause*
>Listen it was
>*Breaks off. Short pause. The Man comes back with a bottle of aqua vita and three soft drink glasses and puts one glass down on the table in front to the Other Man and one down in front of the chair he's been sitting in*

THE MAN
>*To the Woman*
>You want some too
>I suppose
>*He puts a glass down on the table in front of the chair she sits in*

THE WOMAN
>I'd rather have a glass of wine
>*She gets up, goes around the corner of the house and the Man opens the bottle, pours a drink, first to the Other Man, then to himself, he puts the bottle down on the table, and lifts his glass*

THE MAN
>Well
>cheers

The Other Man lifts his glass, they clink their glasses, they drink
I'm glad
you came back
with me
Encouragingly
We must go out on the fjord together
Short pause
And besides
It'd be good to have a look at the boat shed
too
like the old days
The Man empties his glass
Empty your glass
We've got a whole bottle
The Other Man empties his glass and the Man fills both their glasses. The Woman enters from the house with a bottle of wine with an opener screwed into the cork

THE WOMAN

I can't open the bottle
She puts the bottle firmly between her thighs, pulls, but the cork won't loosen. The Other Man gets up, goes over to her

THE OTHER MAN

I'll give you a hand
She gives him the bottle and he pulls out the cork

THE WOMAN

To the Man
Did you see that
He helped me
He opened the bottle for me
The Other Man holds the bottle out to her and she goes to the table, pours herself a glass of wine, sits down in the chair again. The Other Man sits down again on the bench, takes a sip from his glass. She tastes her wine
Good wine

She lifts her glass to the Other Man
Cheers
*They clink their glasses, they drink and put the glasses down on
the table. Long pause*
Well here we are
and there
in front of us
Points to the fjord, jokingly
is the beautiful fjord
and the beautiful mountains
and the beautiful icefloes
Isn't it beautiful

THE MAN
Don't be silly

THE WOMAN
I mean it
To the Other Man
Isn't it beautiful

THE OTHER MAN
Stares ahead of him
I don't know

THE WOMAN
*Starts to laugh.
To the Other Man*
You always say either yes
or no
or perhaps
Or you say
I don't know
The Other Man doesn't look at her

THE MAN
Leave him in peace
Why can't you leave him in peace

THE WOMAN
> *To the Other Man*
> Why don't you play the guitar
> for us
> *He shakes his head*
> Please
> *She takes the guitar, puts it in his lap*
> Come on
> play something
> *He looks with embarrassment at the two of them*
> Oh come on
> *He tries a couple of chords and holds out the guitar to the Man,*
> *who takes it*

THE MAN
> *To the Woman*
> Happy
> now

THE WOMAN
> Why not
> *She drinks her wine. The Other Man drinks from his glass, gets*
> *up*

THE OTHER MAN
> I think I'll

THE WOMAN
> *Interrupts him*
> No you can't leave now

THE MAN
> Stay for a while longer

THE OTHER MAN
> No I should be going
> *He stands and looks down*

THE MAN
> One more glass

THE OTHER MAN
　　I should be going

THE MAN
　　Well let's talk later then
　　We'll be here all summer

THE OTHER MAN
　　Yes we'll talk later

THE MAN
　　And we'll go out on the fjord
　　go out fishing
　　together
　　one evening

THE OTHER MAN
　　Yes

THE MAN
　　And then you can show us the boat shed
　　too
　　right
　　The Other Man nods
　　To the Woman
　　That'd be good
　　right

THE WOMAN
　　As the Other Man exits right
　　Yes
　　She gets up, takes her wine glass and moves into the garden,
　　stands and looks at the fjord. The Man starts to play the tune
　　he remembered earlier. She turns to him
　　Do you always have to play that one
　　Don't you know any other tunes
　　He just continues with his playing. Pause
　　There's your daughter again
　　down on the road
　　with that boy

I don't know his name
they just stand there holding each other
He keeps playing
And now your old friend is walking past them
Short pause
They don't even seem to notice him
They're completely wrapped up
in each other
Come and have a look
He stops playing, takes a sip. The Woman empties her glass,
puts it down on the table
I think I'll go for a walk
The Man nods. She exits right. The Man gets up and walks
into the garden and stands holding the guitar and looking out
on the fjord

Lights down

Blackout

ACT FOUR

Late morning

The Man enters from the house, he's carrying a suitcase, he walks over to the garden table, puts the suitcase down, turns around, looks towards the corner of the house where the Woman enters, she's carrying a bag, and she walks over to the table, puts the bag down next to the suitcase

THE WOMAN
>*Looks at the Man*
>We may as well leave

THE MAN
>If that's what you want
>But it's pretty stupid
>We've only just arrived
>we've only been here a few days
>and now we're leaving again
>*She laughs, either happy or frustrated*

THE WOMAN
>We're leaving

THE MAN
>Yes we may as well
>*Short pause*

THE WOMAN
>What about
>your mother
>Suddenly
>without any warning
>we decide
>we want to leave
>After we've told her
>we're going to stay all summer

we end up staying a couple of days
and then suddenly
we're leaving

THE MAN
Yes

THE WOMAN
Mimics him, questioningly
Yes

THE MAN
A bit cross
Yes

THE WOMAN
You mother's confused
She's been looking forward to this visit
and then
oh well

THE MAN
What brought this on
Breaks off
Do you want to stay
after all
Short pause
We could easily stay a bit longer
I'd like to go out on the fjord once
at least

THE WOMAN
No
we're leaving

THE MAN
That's what we're doing
We're leaving
*The Girl enters from the house, she sits down on a chair, her
legs sprawled in front of her*

THE WOMAN
> *To the Girl*
> You don't want to leave

THE GIRL
> *Cross*
> No
> *The Woman exits into the house*
> *Accusingly, to the Man*
> Why do we have to leave
> already

THE MAN
> We've decided that's all

THE GIRL
> Just when I was beginning to
> like it here
> We were going to stay here
> all summer
> And we've only been here a few days

THE MAN
> Yes I know that

THE GIRL
> And it wasn't me
> who insisted on coming here

THE MAN
> Well it's too late now
> We've already packed

THE GIRL
> I haven't packed

THE MAN
> But we've packed
> your mother and I

THE GIRL
I want to stay here
I don't want to leave
now
It's great to be here
now
Today's got to be the best day
we've had so far
Sunny and warm

THE MAN
A bit teasingly
And then there's this boy
what's his name again

THE GIRL
A bit embarrassed
You don't mind do you
about him

THE MAN
No no
Short pause
What have you done with him

THE GIRL
He's in my room
She gets up

THE MAN
Are you going up to pack

THE GIRL
Do I have to
The Woman enters from the corner of the house, she's carrying a suitcase

THE MAN
To the Girl
Perhaps you can stay a bit longer
if you really want to

I could ask your mother
To the Woman
She doesn't want to go home
*The Woman doesn't answer. The Girl exits into the house and
the Man sits down on the bench*
To the Woman
Is that all then

THE WOMAN
Your guitar's still in there

THE MAN
You're sure you want to leave

THE WOMAN
Yes

THE MAN
You don't want to be here any more

THE WOMAN
A bit irritated
No
The Mother enters from the corner of the house
To the Mother, trying to put the blame on the Man
Well this happened rather
suddenly

THE MOTHER
Yes it did
Short pause
But Siv
She can stay here
if she wants to

THE MAN
Has she asked you

THE MOTHER
No
I just thought
Breaks off

THE MAN
>Well if she wants to
>*To the Woman*
>It's alright isn't it

THE WOMAN
>Yes of course
>*Pause*

THE MOTHER
>But you've got to visit again
>soon

THE MAN
>Yes of course
>*Short pause*
>It's a pity all this
>but
>*The Mother walks around the garden*

THE WOMAN
>*To the Mother*
>So Siv doesn't want to go home

THE MOTHER
>No
>*The Mother looks down towards the fjord, then turns to the Man*
>Look there's Leif again
>He's just standing on the road
>He's looking up
>to the house
>You'd better go down to him
>talk to him
>*Short pause*
>Why don't you go down
>*Short pause. The Man gets up*
>*To the Woman, her voice a bit louder*
>It's a bit strange isn't it
>I hardly ever see him these days

he usually stays inside
his mother does all the shopping
To the Man
You should go down to him
talk to him
The Man exits right. Pause
To the Woman
I feel a bit sorry for Leif
Short pause
He never made anything
of his life
His mother used to worry
about him

THE WOMAN
Yes

THE MOTHER
Half to herself
I don't really know what happened to him
But something did
Short pause
To the Woman
But why do you have to leave
so suddenly
A bit hurt, a bit accusingly
I thought you were going to stay here
all summer
just about

THE WOMAN
Yes me too

THE MOTHER
He's the one who wants to leave

THE WOMAN
Yes you're right
Short pause

THE MOTHER
He's always been
so impulsive
you know

THE WOMAN
Yes

THE MOTHER
Well it was good to see you again

THE WOMAN
It was good to see you too

THE MOTHER
I hope you'll come back again soon

THE WOMAN
Yes we will
Pause. The Mother looks out on the fjord

THE MOTHER
Turns to the Woman
You know
I can't get it out of
my mind
It's just like the old days
when I see Geir and Leif together
I've got to admit
I think it's nice

THE WOMAN
Yes
The Man enters from right, stops, the Other Man appears

THE MOTHER
To the Other Man
Oh isn't this nice
Glad you could drop in again

It's just like the old days
isn't it
I'm feeling young again
almost
She laughs towards the Woman
Funny isn't it
it's just like it used to be
almost
To the Other Man
Why don't you come and sit down
Would you like a cup of coffee
perhaps

THE OTHER MAN
No thank you
The Mother looks at the Man and the Woman
What about you

THE MAN
No thank you

THE WOMAN
No thank you

THE MOTHER
Laughs a little
Alright then
The Mother exits to the house

THE MAN
To the Other Man
We're leaving
now
as you can see
We were going to stay all summer
but
well
it didn't work out like that
We'll have to go out on the fjord together
some other time

The Other Man nods

THE OTHER MAN
Yes

THE MAN
We'll go out on the fjord
for sure
Another time
Another summer
And then I'll go and have a good look at the old shed
again too
That'll be good

THE OTHER MAN
Oh yes

THE MAN
Some other time then

THE WOMAN
To the Other Man
Yes
we're leaving
already
The Girl enters from the house

THE GIRL
I'll stay here
for a while
then
Grandma said I could stay

THE WOMAN
Yes
why don't you

THE MAN
If Grandma says it's
alright

THE GIRL
> She says it's alright with her
> *The Mother enters from the house, carrying a box of chocolates*

THE MOTHER
> *To the Other Man*
> You must have something to eat before you go
> *She holds out the box of chocolates to the Other Man and he takes a piece, then she holds out the box to the Girl, who also takes a piece*

THE GIRL
> Thanks Grandma

THE MOTHER
> Here Geir
> I know
> you'd like one

THE MAN
> Yes thanks
> *The Mother holds out the box of chocolates and he takes a piece*

THE MOTHER
> Hilde
> *The Woman shakes her head*
> *The Other Man sits down on the bench*
> *To the Other Man*
> It's good to see you here again

THE OTHER MAN
> Yes

THE MOTHER
> *To the Girl*
> I'm glad you could stay a bit longer
> now you can keep me company

THE WOMAN
> *To the Mother*
> Thanks for letting her stay

THE MAN
I'll go and get
the guitar
then
The Man exits around the corner of the house

THE MOTHER
To the Woman
Oh it's no trouble

THE WOMAN
To the Other Man
We're going back to town
again
The Other Man nods

THE MOTHER
To the Other Man
They decided very suddenly
They'd hardly got here
before they're off again
A short laugh. Pause

THE WOMAN
To the Other Man
Are you going fishing again this summer

THE OTHER MAN
I guess so

THE MOTHER
Wants to be nice
You do a lot of fishing
don't you Leif

THE OTHER MAN
A fair bit

THE MAN
Keeps you and your mother in fish

THE OTHER MAN
  Oh yes

THE MOTHER
  Have you caught any salmon this season

THE OTHER MAN
  Shakes his head
  No

THE MOTHER
  He's a slippery one
  that salmon
  The Man enters from the house, carrying a guitar case, holding it up

THE MAN
  To the Other Man
  We look like we could be on our way to a gig
  The Other Man nods and the Man puts the guitar case down next to the table

THE WOMAN
  To the Other Man
  Why don't you play something for us
  You didn't get to play
  yesterday

THE OTHER MAN
  Hesitates
  No

THE WOMAN
  Yes

THE OTHER MAN
  I don't play any more

THE WOMAN
  Never

THE OTHER MAN
    No I've stopped

THE MOTHER
    You used to play
    with that teacher
    But you've stopped now have you

THE OTHER MAN
    Yes

THE MAN
    Play something for us
    anyway
    *The Man opens the guitar case, hands the guitar to the Other
    Man, he sits with it in his lap, lets his fingers run over the
    strings*
    Come on Leif
    Play for us
    You can do it
    I know you can do it

THE OTHER MAN
    No

THE MAN
    Of course you can
    The Other Man just sits there with the guitar on his lap
    Just one tune
    *The Other Man fumbles with the guitar for a while, then holds
    it out to the Man*
    You don't want to

THE OTHER MAN
    No I don't feel like it
    The Man takes the guitar. Pause

THE MAN
    To the Woman
    Have we finished packing

THE WOMAN
I've finished
anyway

THE MAN
Me too
The Man stands there holding his guitar, starts playing a tune

THE WOMAN
To the Mother while he plays
Wasn't much of a holiday

THE MOTHER
You'll have to come back again soon

THE WOMAN
Yes

THE GIRL
To the Woman
Are you leaving now

THE WOMAN
Yes
I think we are

THE GIRL
Well
I'll be off
then

THE WOMAN
To the Girl
We're leaving in a minute
I'll give you a call

THE MAN
While he plays. To the Girl
We'll call you tonight

THE GIRL
OK
The Girl exits to the house. The Other Man gets up

THE OTHER MAN
I'd better be getting home
Short pause

THE MAN
Still playing
It was good to see you again

THE WOMAN
Look after yourself then
The Other Man exits right. Pause

THE MOTHER
To the Woman
Strange man
Hardly opens his mouth

THE WOMAN
Yes he's strange
The Man stops playing, bends down and puts the guitar back in the case

THE MAN
As he is getting up again
We'd better start loading up the car

THE MOTHER
There's no rush

THE WOMAN
To the Man
Yes
She takes a suitcase and the bag

THE MAN
To the Woman
We've got everything

THE WOMAN
Yes
The Woman starts to exit right and the Man takes the last
suitcase and the guitar case and follows her out. The Mother
sits down on the bench, takes a piece of chocolate, puts back the
lid on the box. The Girl and the Boy enter from the house. The
Mother picks up the box of chocolates, opens it and holds it out
to the two them

THE MOTHER
Another piece of chocolate

THE GIRL
No thanks

THE MOTHER
To the Boy
What about you

THE BOY
Takes a piece
Yes thank you

THE MOTHER
To the Girl
I'm glad you wanted to stay
She gets up
I'd better
see them off
She exits right. The Girl sits down on the bench

THE GIRL
Looks at the Boy
I don't get it
Short pause
First Dad goes on and on about coming here
we're going to stay here the whole summer
and then
we've only just arrived
and they turn around and go home again
Short pause

THE BOY
And your mother hanging out with him

THE GIRL
No
She doesn't really

THE BOY
Yes she does
And I bet that's why your Dad wants to leave

THE GIRL
No
she's just chatting
flirting a bit
perhaps
just to make Dad jealous
as she says

THE BOY
I saw them
out there
on the island

THE GIRL
Yes
Pause

THE BOY
And him
I mean he's
Breaks off

THE GIRL
It's not like that
Short pause
A little uncertain
You were out
in the boat

THE BOY
>*Questioningly*
>When I saw them

THE GIRL
>*Nods*
>Yes

THE BOY
>Yes

THE GIRL
>So what happened
>you know

THE BOY
>They went behind a mound
>Her breasts
>*He shows with his hands how they wobbled up and down*
>That's all I could see
>*Looks at her*
>No I'm only kidding

THE GIRL
>It's too stupid
>Everything's just crazy
>and it's always been like that
>I don't get it
>It's all so stupid
>*Looks at the Boy*
>Isn't it

THE BOY
>Fancy surprising them
>when they were in the shed
>Does your father know about that

THE GIRL
>I'm sure he doesn't
>*Short pause*
>Perhaps he's

noticed something
I guess that's why he wants to leave
Really it's nothing
not really

THE BOY
It's all so crazy

THE GIRL
And nothing makes sense

THE BOY
No

THE GIRL
It's too stupid
Short pause

THE BOY
It's pretty pointless
God it's pointless

THE GIRL
Starts to laugh
Straight up

THE BOY
Yes straight up

THE GIRL
Yes straight up
She gets up

THE BOY
But doesn't your Dad get jealous

THE GIRL
Maybe
But he just sits there with his
guitar
writing music
no one cares about

THE BOY
I suppose it's one way to kill time

The sound of a car starting and driving away. The Girl and the Boy walks into the garden and she lifts her arm and waves, then he puts his arm around her back and she puts her arm around his back and then they hold both arms around each other, and entwined they kiss each other for a long time

Silence

Lights down

Blackout

DEATH VARIATIONS
(Dødsvariasjonar)

Characters

THE OLDER WOMAN

THE OLDER MAN

THE YOUNG WOMAN

THE YOUNG MAN

THE FRIEND

THE DAUGHTER

THE OLDER WOMAN
Talks to herself
As if it was always there
and never there
and it can never be known
and never be
forsaken
It is a life
with another tranquillity
than the one we're going to see

THE OLDER MAN
Looks at her, wondering
we're going to see

THE OLDER WOMAN
Continues as if he isn't there
And it snatches its opportunities
Short pause
but continues deeper
and deeper
into a night
revealed

THE OLDER MAN
What are you talking about

THE OLDER WOMAN
Continues as if he isn't there
into a night
a transparent connection
where inadequacy reigns
and lets you think
that you understand
what there is to understand

THE OLDER MAN
Wonderingly
That you understand

THE OLDER WOMAN
> *Looks at him*
> Yes that you understand
> *She moves away, looks at him*
> It's so terrible
> I don't understand it
> *He nods*
> That she could
> *Breaks off*

THE OLDER MAN
> *Shakes his head resignedly*
> No
> *Short pause*
> I don't understand it

THE OLDER WOMAN
> We should have done something
> and a long time ago

THE OLDER MAN
> Yes
> *Pause*

THE OLDER WOMAN
> *In despair*
> We've got to do something

THE OLDER MAN
> There's nothing we can do

THE OLDER WOMAN
> Is it too late

THE OLDER MAN
> It's all too late

THE OLDER WOMAN
> Why did she do it

THE OLDER MAN
  I don't understand it

THE OLDER WOMAN
  Our only daughter
  our only
  Breaks off

THE OLDER MAN
  Continues
  Our only child

THE OLDER WOMAN
  But that's not how it is
  it's not possible

THE OLDER MAN
  She followed her death

THE OLDER WOMAN
  Don't say that
  She can't be dead
  that's not how it is
  Short pause

THE OLDER MAN
  She is dead
  She is gone
  forever gone

THE OLDER WOMAN
  She can't be gone
  It's not possible

THE OLDER MAN
  No
  Pause

THE OLDER WOMAN
  How could she

THE OLDER MAN
> *Suddenly*
> Why don't you leave
> I want you to leave

THE OLDER WOMAN
> *Surprised*
> You want me to leave

THE OLDER MAN
> Yes

THE OLDER WOMAN
> But we
> *Short pause*
> well we
> well it's just the two of us left
> now that she's gone

THE OLDER MAN
> You have to leave
> *Short pause*
> because I can't bear
> to see your face
> *She moves away from him*

THE OLDER WOMAN
> I just thought
> you see I had to
> well I had to tell you

THE OLDER MAN
> Yes
> *Short pause*
> But
> well
> well you can't stay here any longer
> You have to leave
> *Pause. The Young Woman, who is pregnant, enters and walks towards the Older Woman, they look at each other*

THE OLDER WOMAN
> *To the Older Man*
> It's all so long ago
> I remember me
> when I was carrying her
> *Short pause*
> But it feels
> well almost as if
> *Short pause*
> it's never happened
> *Short pause*
> Don't you feel like that too
> *He nods. The Young Woman holds her stomach, stands and feels it, and the Friend enters, he looks at the Young Woman, then looks down. The Older Woman and the Older Man look at him, afraid, then they look down*
> I don't want to any more
> *Short pause*
> because everything's a vanishing
> *Short pause*
> I no longer have a reason
> *Pause*
> Stupid thing to say
> *The Young Woman turns around and sees the Young Man who enters and walks towards her, they meet, they embrace, move away from each other, look at each other*
> I don't exist any more
> I don't want to any more

THE YOUNG MAN
> *To the Young Woman*
> Well we're finally here
> wasting our time with that crazy landlord
> *Short pause*
> But now
> *Happy, brings out a set of keys*
> now

Well now we've finally got somewhere to live
Isn't that great

THE YOUNG WOMAN
Yes great
Short pause

THE YOUNG MAN
We've lived
how many places have we
lived
It's more than a few
that's for sure

THE YOUNG WOMAN
An awful lot of places
The Young Man looks at the Older Man, they both look down
and the Young Man looks at the Young Woman, who stands
and looks around

THE YOUNG MAN
This isn't too bad
Short pause
We could easily live here
for a while at least
OK so it's a basement
And I'm sure it's damp and cold
But
well
Short pause
it was all we could get

THE YOUNG WOMAN
I don't think I like it much
well perhaps it's alright
at least when you're here
it'll be alright
yes
She smiles at him
But that awful landlord

Short pause
I hope he won't be pestering us
come knocking on the door
and things

THE YOUNG MAN
Oh it'll be fine

THE YOUNG WOMAN
He just stood there and stared at us
didn't say anything
just stood there
Short pause
And it's expensive
we're paying a small fortune
just for a place to live
We won't be able to afford much else
after we've paid the rent
all we can afford is the rent
Short pause
that man's going to get almost every penny we have
just so we can live
here in his basement

THE YOUNG MAN
It was the only place I could find
I just couldn't
Breaks off

THE YOUNG WOMAN
I'm not blaming you
You did the best you could
I know you did
You tried everything you could
and well
finally you found us
Breaks off

THE YOUNG MAN
>   We don't have to stay here long
>   But we've got to live somewhere
>   *Short pause*
>   and it's not too bad
>   here
>   *Short pause*
>   We can stay here
>   for a while at least

THE YOUNG WOMAN
>   *Puts her hand on her stomach*
>   My stomach seems to grow so fast

THE YOUNG MAN
>   Yes

THE YOUNG WOMAN
>   Incredibly fast

THE YOUNG MAN
>   We're far too young
>   really to have a child

THE YOUNG WOMAN
>   Far too young
>   *Short pause*
>   But when we're stupid enough
>   not to be careful
>   well
>   *Looks at him almost comfortingly*
>   Yes
>   *Almost accusingly*
>   Yes when you don't know how to be careful
>   well
>   *Short pause*
>   I'm sure my grandmother
>   would've had a word of wisdom about that
>   What did she use to say

something about it doesn't pay
an expression

THE YOUNG MAN
But you can't remember it

THE YOUNG WOMAN
No it's gone

THE YOUNG MAN
Something about the punishment fits the crime

THE YOUNG WOMAN
Perhaps
yes something like that

THE YOUNG MAN
It'll all work out
you'll see
Pause

THE YOUNG WOMAN
But we've hardly got any money

THE YOUNG MAN
Well that stupid landlord
wanted rent in advance
and everything else he could think of
and now

THE YOUNG WOMAN
Continues
and now we've hardly got any money left

THE YOUNG MAN
Just a little

THE YOUNG WOMAN
Very little

THE YOUNG MAN
Almost nothing

THE YOUNG WOMAN
And what are we going to do

THE YOUNG MAN
I have to try to find a job

THE YOUNG WOMAN
I could try that
as well

THE YOUNG MAN
You

THE YOUNG WOMAN
Yes

THE YOUNG MAN
You
in your condition

THE YOUNG WOMAN
Yes

THE YOUNG MAN
Don't be stupid
Pause

THE YOUNG WOMAN
So I'll have to sit here alone
In the basement below that landlord
hour after hour
while you're gone
doing some kind of job

THE YOUNG MAN
I'm sure I won't find a job

THE YOUNG WOMAN
Then we won't have any money

THE YOUNG MAN
No

THE YOUNG WOMAN
But we've got some

THE YOUNG MAN
Some
not much
we've got
some money
Short pause
But we'll be alright

THE YOUNG WOMAN
How can you be so sure
We've hardly got anything
No possessions
No money

THE YOUNG MAN
But we've got each other
And we're young

THE YOUNG WOMAN
It's not a lot

THE YOUNG MAN
It's enough

THE YOUNG WOMAN
How do you know

THE YOUNG MAN
I just know
Short pause
We'll be alright

THE YOUNG WOMAN
If you say so
Short pause
But I'm so worried

THE YOUNG MAN
  We're young and strong

THE YOUNG WOMAN
  Don't be silly

THE YOUNG MAN
  It's true

THE YOUNG WOMAN
  It's all so uncertain

THE YOUNG MAN
  Well that's life

THE YOUNG WOMAN
  I'm so scared and worried

THE YOUNG MAN
  Don't be scared
  Please
  He puts his arms around her, holds her

THE OLDER MAN
  To the Older Woman
  It's not possible
  That's not how it is

THE OLDER WOMAN
  No
  Short pause
  She can't be gone

THE FRIEND
  She's gone

THE OLDER WOMAN
  To the Older Man
  Our only child
  She
  Short pause
  no she

my only child
no she can't be gone

THE OLDER MAN
It's not possible

THE FRIEND
She's no longer with you
She's with me

THE OLDER WOMAN
To the Older Man
Still that's how it is
Short pause
I saw her lying there
Short pause
They called me
asked me to come
asked me to come and see her

THE OLDER MAN
It's not how it is

THE OLDER WOMAN
I saw her
she was lying there
I had to go and see her

THE OLDER MAN
When I see your face
Breaks off

THE OLDER WOMAN
Yes

THE OLDER MAN
Your face
Short pause
I can't bear
to see your face

THE OLDER WOMAN
I had to go there
They rang

THE OLDER MAN
Your eyes

THE OLDER WOMAN
And she was just lying there

THE OLDER MAN
In a low voice
Your face

THE OLDER WOMAN
She was lying there
Pause
But I'll go now
I'll
Breaks off
Yes
yes I think
I'll go
Short pause
But I had to
Short pause
well I had to come
had to tell you
had to let you know
yes
But I'll go now

THE OLDER MAN
She was just lying there

THE OLDER WOMAN
And her hair
And her face
Her face
She wasn't there any more
she wasn't in her face any more

THE OLDER MAN
>Her face was empty
>*Pause*
>Why don't you leave

THE FRIEND
>Just leave

THE OLDER MAN
>*Continues*
>you see I can't bear
>*Breaks off*
>Leave
>Please just leave

THE OLDER WOMAN
>Do you think she wanted to do it

THE FRIEND
>She wanted to be with me
>She's here
>with me
>She's with me now

THE OLDER MAN
>No
>*Short pause*
>she just did it
>It just happened

THE OLDER WOMAN
>She just did it
>she didn't know what she did

THE OLDER MAN
>It doesn't make any difference
>It can't be undone

THE FRIEND
>She's with me now

THE OLDER MAN
>*To the Older Woman*
>Please can't you
>it's as if
>well I can't any longer
>*Breaks off. He looks at the Young Man*

THE YOUNG MAN
>*To the Young Woman*
>There's no need
>to be scared
>*Short pause*
>because
>well
>you look so worried
>but you mustn't be scared
>I'll look after you
>I will
>always
>I'll be your friend
>I will
>You know that don't you

THE OLDER MAN
>*To himself*
>Everything's finished

THE OLDER WOMAN
>Now I've told you

THE YOUNG MAN
>I'll always be
>your friend
>through the years
>through the days
>I'll be there for you
>in your night
>in your days
>*Short pause*

I'm so glad
I've met you

THE OLDER WOMAN
To herself
And it reveals itself
and vanishes
and
Breaks off

THE YOUNG MAN
Now
that I've met you
I can rest
I can sleep
Now
yes
everything's better now
so don't be afraid of anything
please
don't be afraid

THE YOUNG WOMAN
Questioningly
Nothing bad is going to happen any more

THE YOUNG MAN
No
nothing

THE YOUNG WOMAN
Are you sure about that

THE YOUNG MAN
Yes I'm sure

THE YOUNG WOMAN
Laughs happily
Alright then

THE YOUNG MAN
>   *Questioningly, teases*
>   So
>   it's alright then

THE YOUNG WOMAN
>   Yes it is
>   *Pause*
>   And now it's not

THE YOUNG MAN
>   *Continues*
>   too long till the baby's due
>   right
>   that's what you were going to say
>   right
>   *She nods*
>   How long is it
>   A few weeks

THE YOUNG WOMAN
>   Till it's due
>   well it's
>   *Thinks*
>   it's
>   yes it's seven days

THE YOUNG MAN
>   *Surprised*
>   Seven days

THE YOUNG WOMAN
>   Had you forgotten

THE YOUNG MAN
>   I'm so bad with dates
>   *Short pause*
>   I can't remember numbers
>   I only just manage
>   to remember my own birthday

But any other number
Breaks off

THE YOUNG WOMAN
A little disappointed
Well you could try to remember
this one at least

THE YOUNG MAN
I do remember
I just don't
I mean
not the exact day
Short pause
you know I've got
a lot on my mind
don't you

THE YOUNG WOMAN
Yes I know

THE YOUNG MAN
So don't be angry with me

THE YOUNG WOMAN
I'm not angry with you
Pause
It was good
of your parents
to lend us some money

THE YOUNG MAN
Yes

THE YOUNG WOMAN
It's not as if they have
a lot
to spare

THE YOUNG MAN
>No
>*Short pause*
>If I hadn't been able to borrow
>a little from them
>I don't know what

THE YOUNG WOMAN
>No what would we've done then

THE YOUNG MAN
>I've no idea
>*Short pause*
>Let's not think about that
>We're together now
>and we've got a place of our own
>We've even got
>a little money

THE YOUNG WOMAN
>Yes

THE YOUNG MAN
>Everything's fine

THE YOUNG WOMAN
>Yes
>Oh
>listen
>My stomach
>feels tight
>here
>*She touches her stomach, looks at him*

THE YOUNG MAN
>It feels tight

THE YOUNG WOMAN
>*Grimaces*
>It's getting worse

It's getting tighter
Oh
I think
Breaks off

THE YOUNG MAN
Is it the baby
Is the baby coming

THE FRIEND
The baby's coming

THE YOUNG WOMAN
I think it's
Breaks off, grimaces

THE YOUNG MAN
We should
shouldn't we
well let's
Breaks off

THE YOUNG WOMAN
I think it's a contraction
and that
that
Breaks off

THE YOUNG MAN
We've got to go to the hospital

THE YOUNG WOMAN
Yes

THE YOUNG MAN
But

THE YOUNG WOMAN
You've got to get a car

THE YOUNG MAN
Yes

THE YOUNG WOMAN
Bends over with the pain
You've got to call

THE YOUNG MAN
Yes

THE YOUNG WOMAN
Moans
Yes
Short pause
It hurts so much

THE YOUNG MAN
It hurts
It really hurts now
Pause

THE YOUNG WOMAN
Not right now
I feel nothing right now
nothing at all
nothing
Short pause
It comes and goes

THE YOUNG MAN
Yes
Short pause

THE YOUNG WOMAN
But I'm sure I've got contractions
I think the baby's coming

THE YOUNG MAN
We've got to
Breaks off

THE YOUNG WOMAN
Yes I think you've got to get a car
I can't take the bus

you know
Laughs briefly and uncertainly

THE YOUNG MAN
No
no of course not
Short pause
Perhaps I
yes
yes perhaps I could
yes I could go to him
to the landlord
I could ask to borrow his phone

THE YOUNG WOMAN
If you dare to

THE YOUNG MAN
Yes
He remains where he is, and she has a new contraction, and she grimaces
I'm going

THE YOUNG WOMAN
Hurry up

THE YOUNG MAN
Yes I'll hurry

THE YOUNG WOMAN
Hurry
Please
He starts to leave
No wait
I'll come with you
Couldn't I
Breaks off

THE YOUNG MAN
    Yes
    if you want to
    of course

THE YOUNG WOMAN
    come
    The pain is coming
    with you
    He puts his arm around her shoulders

THE OLDER MAN
    Yes
    it's
    Breaks off. Pause
    And now she's gone
    Short pause
    gone forever
    The Young Man and the Young Woman leave

THE OLDER WOMAN
    Don't talk about it
    I was feeling good
    just now
    I saw her in my mind
    as I cradled her
    in my arms
    Short pause
    And I see her
    Points
    totter around on the floor
    with her black hair
    her long black hair
    I see the child I bore
    walk around
    in her raincoat
    in the wild rain

THE OLDER MAN
    Stamping her little feet in the mud

THE OLDER WOMAN
Stamping with all her strength
She loved doing that

THE OLDER MAN
She was such a lovely girl
So good
Short pause
and at first she didn't have any hair at all
and then she got
all that long black hair

THE OLDER WOMAN
And she was such a kind girl

THE OLDER MAN
Always
She was so undemanding
never asked for anything
always happy over anything we gave her
Short pause
And she loved
her food
When she was little
She liked
everything we gave her
ate and laughed
and ate some more
Short pause
And when she got older she used to sit
with her feet tucked under her
sit there and read
Short pause
Hour after hour
she'd sit and read

THE OLDER WOMAN
That's what she did more than anything
she'd read and read

Pause
But don't just stand there

THE OLDER MAN
No
Pause

THE OLDER WOMAN
I had to come
I had to tell you

THE OLDER MAN
Yes
*Pause. The Young Woman enters, her stomach has disappeared,
she is somewhat older, she stands and looks around, and the
Friend looks at her*

THE FRIEND
Good
to see you
The Young Woman looks around

THE OLDER MAN
She didn't really like to play
with the other kids

THE OLDER WOMAN
She was so easily frightened
Any sign of rough and tumble
and she'd want to go home

THE YOUNG WOMAN
Shouts
Are you there

THE DAUGHTER
Off stage
Yes what is it

THE YOUNG WOMAN
Come here
Please

The Daughter enters
You can't just
sit alone in your room

THE DAUGHTER
No

THE YOUNG WOMAN
I mean it

THE DAUGHTER
Yes

THE YOUNG WOMAN
Really I don't know
what to say to you
You've got to do something

THE DAUGHTER
Yes
Pause

THE YOUNG WOMAN
You can't just stay at home

THE DAUGHTER
No

THE YOUNG WOMAN
I don't want to hurt you
I only want what's best for you
Short pause
You too have a future
you know
and that means
well you've got to go to school
like everyone else
The Friend comes closer

THE DAUGHTER
Yes
yes you're right

THE YOUNG WOMAN
But you don't like school

THE DAUGHTER
No

THE YOUNG WOMAN
Why not

THE DAUGHTER
I don't really know

THE YOUNG WOMAN
Is it too noisy
or something

THE DAUGHTER
Yes

THE YOUNG WOMAN
Yes it probably is

THE DAUGHTER
Shuffles
Yes

THE FRIEND
To the Daughter
Good to see you

THE DAUGHTER
To the Friend
Yes
Happily
good to see you too

THE FRIEND
But do we know each other
Have we met before

THE DAUGHTER
We have haven't we

THE OLDER WOMAN
To the Daughter, anxiously
No don't
Don't you see
You have to be careful
You shouldn't
Short pause
you shouldn't talk to him

THE DAUGHTER
To the Friend
Yes
Good to see you

THE FRIEND
Maybe
yes maybe we know each other
Maybe we've known each other a long time

THE DAUGHTER
I think so

THE FRIEND
Yes
that's right
maybe
we know each other
yes maybe we do

THE DAUGHTER
Oh I think we do

THE FRIEND
Yes we do
Pause
I hope you're well

THE DAUGHTER
Quite well
thanks
Pause

THE FRIEND
You've got lovely hair
long and black

THE DAUGHTER
You think so

THE FRIEND
Yes
really lovely
Pause
But where have we
well met each other before

THE DAUGHTER
I'm not sure

THE FRIEND
Or maybe we've just always
known each other
Maybe that's how it is

THE DAUGHTER
Yes maybe it is

THE FRIEND
I think we've always known each other

THE DAUGHTER
Maybe we have
Short pause

THE FRIEND
I have to go now

THE DAUGHTER
But you're coming back

THE FRIEND
Yes

THE DAUGHTER
You'll be back

THE FRIEND
Yes
yes I could come back

THE DAUGHTER
You promise

THE FRIEND
Yes
He starts to leave

THE DAUGHTER
Follows him
Promise you will

THE FRIEND
Yes
He leaves, and the Daughter follows him out. Pause

THE OLDER MAN
She was such a good girl

THE OLDER WOMAN
And so gentle

THE OLDER MAN
So good and gentle
Short pause

THE OLDER WOMAN
And we kept living there
And the days passed
the years passed
Short pause
and then she moved out
And I hardly saw her any more

Pause
She's got to be here
She can't just disappear

THE OLDER MAN
No
she's here
She's got to be here still
Pause. The Older Woman moves away from the Older Man,
turns and looks at him

THE OLDER WOMAN
I'm leaving now
Short pause
You said you didn't want to see me any more
and I can leave now
Short pause
You said you didn't want to see my face
The Young Man enters, he, too, is somewhat older, he stops,
looks down and the Young Woman looks at him

THE OLDER MAN
I don't know what it is
about your face
Short pause
I can't bear looking at it
Short pause
You're not in your face
any more
Your eyes
are no longer your eyes
they are
Breaks off

THE OLDER WOMAN
That's just how things turned out
The Young Man just stands there, as if he is disappearing into
himself

THE YOUNG WOMAN
To the Young Man
What's the matter

THE YOUNG MAN
No
it's nothing
Pause

THE YOUNG WOMAN
So everything's alright

THE YOUNG MAN
Yes
Why do you ask

THE YOUNG WOMAN
There's something about you

THE YOUNG MAN
Something about me

THE YOUNG WOMAN
It's
Short pause
as if you're somewhere else

THE YOUNG MAN
Don't be silly

THE YOUNG WOMAN
No
I just thought
well if something's the matter
you know you can tell me
that's all

THE YOUNG MAN
No nothing's the matter
Pause

THE YOUNG WOMAN
You're sure

THE YOUNG MAN
Yes
Pause

THE YOUNG WOMAN
Well I won't ask

THE YOUNG MAN
Nothing's the matter
Why do you keep asking

THE YOUNG WOMAN
I don't know
You're just a bit
quiet
you don't say anything
you sort of
live inside yourself

THE YOUNG MAN
Nothing's the matter
Why do you carry on about it

THE YOUNG WOMAN
Look I know there's something

THE YOUNG MAN
No
I'm telling you, it's nothing

THE YOUNG WOMAN
Don't you love me any more

THE YOUNG MAN
A little exasperated
Yes
Pause

THE YOUNG WOMAN
　　Look I know there's something
　　He moves away from her

THE YOUNG WOMAN
　　Talks to his back
　　Where are you going

THE YOUNG MAN
　　Just out for a walk

THE YOUNG WOMAN
　　Can't you stay
　　You're hardly ever at home any more
　　Do you always have to go out

THE YOUNG MAN
　　Turns
　　No I can stay at home

THE YOUNG WOMAN
　　But
　　can't you tell me
　　Short pause
　　well what's the matter

THE YOUNG MAN
　　Nothing

THE YOUNG WOMAN
　　Don't lie to me
　　I know
　　What is it

THE YOUNG MAN
　　Why don't you give it a rest
　　He moves further away from her

THE YOUNG WOMAN
　　Moves after him
　　Where are you going

THE YOUNG MAN
    I'm going to bed

THE YOUNG WOMAN
    Don't you want to spend
    some time with me

THE YOUNG MAN
    Yes
    But I'm tired

THE YOUNG WOMAN
    Don't you want to be with me any more
    you're never at home
    Don't you like me
    Don't you love me any more

THE YOUNG MAN
    It's not that

THE YOUNG WOMAN
    What is it
    then

THE YOUNG MAN
    It's just that I'm tired
    I need to get some sleep

THE YOUNG WOMAN
    Tell me what it is

THE YOUNG MAN
    It's nothing
    Pause

THE YOUNG WOMAN
    Yes it's something
    She grabs his arm
    I can feel it
    Tell me what it is
    What's her name
    Tell me

THE YOUNG MAN
Are you sure you want to know

THE YOUNG WOMAN
Yes
She lets go of his arm. Pause
Tell me her name

THE YOUNG MAN
It's not like that
don't be silly

THE YOUNG WOMAN
Oh I understand
just tell me her name

THE YOUNG MAN
It's not like that

THE YOUNG WOMAN
Don't lie
I understand
I'm not stupid
I understand that much

THE YOUNG MAN
No
it's not like that

THE YOUNG WOMAN
I understand that much

THE YOUNG MAN
Alright
then
She seems to fall apart. Short pause
It is
Breaks off
Well
Well now you know
Can I go to bed now

THE YOUNG WOMAN
Nods
Yes

THE YOUNG MAN
Alright

THE YOUNG WOMAN
Yes you can go to bed now
No don't go
He leaves

THE OLDER WOMAN
To herself
And
yes it glows
Short pause
of something that vanishes
But remains
all the same
To the Older Man
That's true isn't it

THE OLDER MAN
Yes

THE OLDER WOMAN
Everything's gone
And nothing's left
But still
yes
Short pause
yes it's still there
as something else
in a sense

THE OLDER MAN
It's
Breaks off

THE OLDER WOMAN
    You can't just stand there

THE OLDER MAN
    No
    Pause

THE OLDER WOMAN
    I can't quite
    bring myself
    to leave either
    Pause

THE YOUNG WOMAN
    Shouts
    Where are you
    Please come in here
    She wanders around

THE DAUGHTER
    Off stage
    Yes

THE YOUNG WOMAN
    Please come in here to me

THE DAUGHTER
    Off stage
    Yes
    alright

THE YOUNG WOMAN
    Well where
    are you

THE DAUGHTER
    Enters
    Here I am
    She stops
    I was just going to
    Breaks off

THE YOUNG WOMAN
You're always just going to
Short pause
do something or other
Come here

THE DAUGHTER
I'm here now
Pause

THE YOUNG WOMAN
You always say you're coming
and then you don't come

THE DAUGHTER
I'm here
*She and the Young Woman move towards each other, embrace
each other, let go of each other*
But what's the matter with you
Are you sad
What is it

THE YOUNG WOMAN
Nothing

THE DAUGHTER
Don't be silly
I can see it
I can see something's the matter
You're sad

THE YOUNG WOMAN
It's nothing

THE DAUGHTER
No tell me
Tell me what it is

THE YOUNG WOMAN
It's nothing
Pause
Where have you been

THE DAUGHTER
    I just went out
    for a walk
    and then
    well I was in my room now
    But you know that
    Pause
    Where's Dad

THE YOUNG WOMAN
    What did you do when you were out

THE DAUGHTER
    I went for a walk
    that's all

THE YOUNG WOMAN
    No

THE DAUGHTER
    Yes as usual
    Pause
    But what is it

THE YOUNG WOMAN
    It's nothing

THE DAUGHTER
    Alright
    then
    As if she finds it difficult to ask
    Where's Dad
    Why isn't Dad here

THE YOUNG WOMAN
    He'll be here
    he'll be here soon

THE DAUGHTER
    Is he away
    where is he

He's been gone so long
where is he

THE YOUNG WOMAN
He'll be here soon

THE DAUGHTER
Why can't you tell me
where he is

THE YOUNG WOMAN
You should go and do your homework

THE DAUGHTER
I've done it

THE YOUNG WOMAN
That's
good
Pause

THE DAUGHTER
What is it
What's the matter with you
Why are you sad
Why can't you tell me

THE YOUNG WOMAN
It's nothing
Pause

THE DAUGHTER
I think I'll go to bed

THE YOUNG WOMAN
No don't go
stay here
stay with me

THE DAUGHTER
I can't just stay in here
you don't tell me anything
anyway

THE YOUNG WOMAN
No
Smiles at her
no I suppose I don't
I suppose I'm just here
The Friend enters, stops, looks at the Daughter

THE DAUGHTER
But then
yes
Looks at the Friend

THE OLDER WOMAN
To the Older Man
Why
well
why are you just standing there
Short pause
Don't stand there like that
so still
like you're almost
rooted to the spot
don't stand there like that
The Young Man enters

THE OLDER MAN
No
Pause

THE OLDER WOMAN
I'm leaving now
But I had to
Breaks off

THE DAUGHTER
Sees the Young Man walking towards her and runs to him
Hi
there you are
Pause

Well
where have you been
you've been gone so long
where have you been

THE YOUNG MAN
Oh
Short pause
nowhere

THE DAUGHTER
Please tell me
where you've been
Short pause
Did you bring me
a present
Did you
Short pause
the way you used to
when I was a little girl

THE YOUNG MAN
No
Perhaps I should
Breaks off

THE DAUGHTER
But tell me
tell me where you've been
I've been waiting for you

THE YOUNG MAN
No I
Hesitates
No
I've just
Breaks off

THE YOUNG WOMAN
She's been waiting and waiting for you

THE DAUGHTER
Where have you been
tell me
you've got to tell me

THE YOUNG WOMAN
Have you come to get your things

THE DAUGHTER
Puzzled
His things
Get his things
why

THE FRIEND
He's come to get his things

THE YOUNG WOMAN
He's moving out
Your Dad's moving out

THE FRIEND
He's moving out

THE DAUGHTER
You're moving out
No
You're pulling my leg

THE YOUNG WOMAN
Say something
It's up to you to tell her

THE YOUNG MAN
Well I'm
Breaks off
Well your Mum and I
Breaks off

THE DAUGHTER
You're not moving out
You're staying here

with me
with us

THE YOUNG WOMAN
Tell her
tell her how it is

THE YOUNG MAN
Yes
Short pause
at least for a while
I'm going to
well
well I
I
well I'm going to live for a while
by myself
your Mum and I have

THE YOUNG WOMAN
Interrupts him
Your Mum and I
Tell her the truth

THE DAUGHTER
No

THE YOUNG MAN
To the Daughter
But you can visit me
as often as you want to
if you want to

THE YOUNG WOMAN
Interrupts him
She's living with me

THE YOUNG MAN
Yes you should
That's for the best
perhaps

THE DAUGHTER
No
We're going to live here
together
all of us

THE FRIEND
To the Daughter
I'm your friend

THE YOUNG WOMAN
That won't be possible
Short pause
because Dad
well he's fallen in love with someone else

THE DAUGHTER
Someone else

THE YOUNG WOMAN
Your Dad can't live here
with us any more
Pause

THE DAUGHTER
I can help you pack

THE YOUNG MAN
Thank you
That's very nice of you
Why don't we make a start
then
you and I

THE DAUGHTER
Yes let's

THE YOUNG MAN
You're so good
You're the best in the whole world

THE DAUGHTER
But you're going to move out

THE YOUNG MAN
Looks like it
But it's good of you to help me

THE DAUGHTER
I can pack your shirts

THE YOUNG MAN
Yes that'd be good
*The Young Woman leaves and the Friend follows her, stops
and watches her exit, he remains standing, looking down*

THE DAUGHTER
And your socks

THE YOUNG MAN
What a very nice girl you are
You're my best friend

THE DAUGHTER
And your books
I'm sure you want to take a few books

THE YOUNG MAN
Yes it'd be nice
to have a few books

THE DAUGHTER
I'll pack them

THE YOUNG MAN
But I don't need to take all that much
because perhaps
Breaks off

THE DAUGHTER
Continues
Perhaps you won't be away for too long

THE YOUNG MAN
>Perhaps
>*Pause*

THE DAUGHTER
>Yes you've got to come back
>soon
>*Short pause*
>Still you've got to take
>a few books
>a few clothes
>and a few other things
>I'll help you
>I'll help you pack
>*Short pause*
>Just tell me
>tell me what you want me to pack

THE YOUNG MAN
>*Suddenly*
>Listen

THE DAUGHTER
>Yes

THE YOUNG MAN
>Why don't I leave it for a while
>There's no rush
>*Short pause*
>I have to go

THE DAUGHTER
>Yes

THE YOUNG MAN
>Yes it's time to go

THE DAUGHTER
>But come back soon

THE FRIEND
> *To the Daughter*
> I'll be with you

THE YOUNG MAN
> Yes
> *He leaves*

THE DAUGHTER
> Wait
> *She follows him out*

THE OLDER WOMAN
> *To the Older Man*
> I don't want to see you again
> I never want to see you again

THE OLDER MAN
> She was such a lovely
> girl

THE OLDER WOMAN
> We're going to leave each other now
> and we'll never
> see each other again

THE FRIEND
> Just disappear
> from each other

THE OLDER MAN
> *Towards the Older Woman*
> Yes
> *Pause*
> It vanishes
> and returns

THE OLDER WOMAN
> *Questioningly*
> Vanishes and returns

THE OLDER MAN
> We have to leave each other
> *Pause*
> But I miss her so much
> I think about her
> always
> I'll always think about her

THE OLDER WOMAN
> She is here all the time

THE FRIEND
> She is with me now

THE OLDER MAN
> Even if she is gone
> she is here

THE OLDER WOMAN
> She is here
> *Pause*
> And I am alone
> *Short pause*
> and I'll be alone

THE OLDER MAN
> You don't have to be alone

THE OLDER WOMAN
> I want to be alone

THE OLDER MAN
> It's not good for you
> to be alone

THE OLDER WOMAN
> I want to
> I want to be alone

THE OLDER MAN
> It's not good for you

THE OLDER WOMAN
I want to be alone
now that she's
Breaks off. Short pause
She too just vanished

THE OLDER MAN
Almost to himself
I can't bear it

THE OLDER WOMAN
What did you say

THE OLDER MAN
No
nothing

THE OLDER WOMAN
I had to come
I had to tell you

THE OLDER MAN
Yes
Pause. The Daughter enters, a good deal older

THE OLDER WOMAN
To the Older Man
I'll leave now
Pause
I had to
yes
yes you had to know
Breaks off
they
they called me
asked me to come and see
well if it was her

THE DAUGHTER
Sees the Friend
There you are

It's good to see you again
I've thought about you often

THE FRIEND
Do we know each other

THE DAUGHTER
Jokingly
Yes
of course we do
we've always known each other
haven't we

THE FRIEND
Maybe

THE DAUGHTER
Now we know each other
we do now at least

THE FRIEND
Maybe
and maybe we have

THE DAUGHTER
Continues
always known each other

THE FRIEND
But you shouldn't be with me
It's not good for you

THE DAUGHTER
Why not

THE FRIEND
It isn't
Short pause
I have to go now

THE DAUGHTER
Disappointed

Why
It was good to see each other
wasn't it

THE FRIEND
Yes

THE DAUGHTER
We do know each other
you and I

THE FRIEND
Yes
but
Short pause
you shouldn't
you mustn't
like me

THE DAUGHTER
Why not

THE FRIEND
Hesitates
Well

THE DAUGHTER
A little happy
After all my years
Short pause
What do I mean by that
All my years
Short pause
maybe that it's lasted a long time

THE FRIEND
You don't know me
or do you

THE DAUGHTER
I know you

THE FRIEND
Maybe you know me

THE DAUGHTER
Yes
I must
because when I lie there
after all my years
in my bed
Short pause
and it's evening
it's night
now and then
you lie there
yes you seem to lie there
next to me
Short pause
and we just lie there
and rest
we lie there
quietly
calmly
almost dignified
we lie there

THE FRIEND
You don't know me
that's not how I am

THE DAUGHTER
And it's
calm
a calm rest
like sitting and watching the sea
just sitting there
watching the sea
we lie there
so calmly

next to each other
in bed
that's what I think
when I lie there
at night

THE FRIEND
You shouldn't like me

THE DAUGHTER
Shouldn't I
Short pause
Don't you like me

THE FRIEND
Yes

THE DAUGHTER
Can you feel me lying there next to you

THE FRIEND
Yes
Surprised
that's just how it is

THE DAUGHTER
After all my years
Wonder what I mean by that

THE FRIEND
We don't know each other

THE DAUGHTER
We're close to each other
And so far away
from each other

THE FRIEND
We're both far away from each other
And very close to each other
That's how it is
The Young Woman enters

THE DAUGHTER
    Yes

THE FRIEND
    And there's a kind of peace in that
    a sense of great peace
    isn't there

THE DAUGHTER
    Yes

THE FRIEND
    You're a good and kind girl

THE DAUGHTER
    And it's good to know you're lying there
    next to me
    that you're always lying there
    just lying there

THE OLDER WOMAN
    To the Daughter
    You mustn't
    It's dangerous
    Don't you understand

THE DAUGHTER
    To the Friend
    And I'll tell you this
    I don't want to know you
    not you either
    But
    Breaks off

THE FRIEND
    You are lovely

THE DAUGHTER
    I don't want disharmony
    I want harmony

THE OLDER WOMAN
To the Daughter
You mustn't
please don't listen to him
You have to be careful

THE FRIEND
Maybe I am
well
fond of
you
Short pause
or something
anyway

THE DAUGHTER
Because I too need someone
Everyone has their secret
their imagined calm
when they're resting
just resting
in each other
Pause
But I want to be alone
always be alone

THE OLDER WOMAN
To the Daughter
You mustn't
Don't you understand

THE DAUGHTER
To the Friend
We exist within our love
Short pause
But I could never live in our love
It's not possible
The Young Man enters, looks at the Young Woman, who turns away

THE FRIEND
>It's possible
>Everything's possible

THE DAUGHTER
>It's not possible
>I wouldn't dare
>I'm not able to
>That's not how I am
>*Short pause*
>But you are good to rest against
>when you're not aware
>when you're just lying there
>far away
>when you are whoever it is you are
>then you're good
>and calm
>when you are like a sea
>to think about
>to look at
>then you're good
>when you're far away
>*Short pause*
>and at the same time so close

THE FRIEND
>Maybe I'm missing you

THE YOUNG MAN
>*Walks towards the Young Woman*
>We have to talk
>*Short pause*
>She doesn't want to live with you any more

THE YOUNG WOMAN
>No
>she says she wants to move out
>live on her own

THE YOUNG MAN
> She could of course
> *Short pause*
> but she's so young

THE YOUNG WOMAN
> I can't stop her
> She has to do what she wants
> *Short pause*
> But
> well
> well I don't quite understand it
> She
> *Breaks off*

THE YOUNG MAN
> What were you going to say

THE YOUNG WOMAN
> Just that
> well that she's so alone
> she doesn't have any friends
> not that I know of
> anyway
> not a single friend
> no girlfriend
> no boyfriend
> no one

THE YOUNG MAN
> She has mostly kept to herself

THE YOUNG WOMAN
> She's too shy
> or whatever it is

THE YOUNG MAN
> But then
> living on her own
> she'll be even more alone
> won't she

THE YOUNG WOMAN
I can't stop her
not if she wants to

THE YOUNG MAN
Yes of course
Pause

THE DAUGHTER
Walks towards the Young Man and the Young Woman
You're standing there talking
I see

THE YOUNG MAN
Yes
it looks like it
Short pause
Well are you quite sure
you want to live on your own

THE DAUGHTER
Yes
yes I've made up my mind

THE YOUNG MAN
And have you found somewhere to live

THE DAUGHTER
Yes
Pause

THE YOUNG WOMAN
Well if you've made up your mind
there's not much I can say
Short pause
But if you want to live with me
continue to stay here
you're welcome

THE YOUNG MAN
Yes

And you can live with me too
if you want

THE DAUGHTER
With you and that woman
No I don't want that
I couldn't stand that

THE YOUNG MAN
But you could
if you want

THE DAUGHTER
No I want
I want to live on my own

THE YOUNG WOMAN
Yes that's fine too

THE DAUGHTER
Yes that's what I want
Pause. She moves away from them, discovers the Friend

THE DAUGHTER
Good to see you again

THE FRIEND
Yes

THE DAUGHTER
I've missed you

THE FRIEND
You mustn't miss me

THE DAUGHTER
You're good to snuggle up against
and calm
you are
as calm as the sea
yes you are

THE FRIEND
Maybe

THE DAUGHTER
Yes and often
Short pause
well it's as if my heart
surrounds you
or it's
yes it's as if
Short pause
as if my heart is fuller
than itself
and in that fullness
that's where you are
or not you
of course
but it's still you
who are there
Short pause. She and the Friend move towards each other
And for you
how is it for you

THE FRIEND
You shouldn't think about me

THE DAUGHTER
It's not like that for you
Pause
Say something to me

THE FRIEND
I don't know what to say

THE DAUGHTER
Just say something

THE FRIEND
I've got nothing to say
He starts to move away from her. The Daughter continues to speak to him, he turns around, looks at her

THE DAUGHTER
No
don't go
He stops and she smiles at him, as if saying they now have to agree on something, as if saying to him that this is something they both understand, as if this is something simple
But
Breaks off
And then I ask about you
say your name

THE FRIEND
Puzzled
Say my name

THE DAUGHTER
Yes
yes I say your name
Short pause

THE FRIEND
I don't know what to say
He moves away from her, turns to her
Well
I'll be going
then

THE DAUGHTER
Follows him
No listen
He stops and they remain standing and looking at each other, then they move away from each other and he turns and looks at her
Why are you so far away

THE FRIEND
I have to be this far away
And then I have to go

THE DAUGHTER
No don't go

THE FRIEND
And then we can't ever again
Breaks off. Pause
Because love is always hiding itself

THE DAUGHTER
Yes hiding itself
and then showing itself
quite suddenly

THE FRIEND
Yes
Pause

THE FRIEND
I have to go now

THE DAUGHTER
Disappointed
No don't go
Pause
I am scared

THE FRIEND
Don't be scared

THE DAUGHTER
I'm so confused

THE FRIEND
I have to go

THE DAUGHTER
No
don't disappear

THE FRIEND
I have to go

THE DAUGHTER
No don't go

THE OLDER WOMAN
To the Daughter
You mustn't

THE FRIEND
I think it's best
Breaks off

THE OLDER WOMAN
To the Daughter
You must be careful
Don't you understand
You mustn't
Please don't do it

THE FRIEND
Towards the Daughter
Maybe I should go

THE DAUGHTER
I already miss you
Pause. She looks around and starts to walk towards the Older Woman

THE OLDER WOMAN
To the Daughter
What a surprise
It's good of you to drop in
It's a long time since
Short pause
But I suppose you're very busy
It's been a long time
since I've seen you
How are things

THE DAUGHTER
Good thanks

THE OLDER WOMAN
Good
that's good

THE DAUGHTER
Yes
everything's fine

THE OLDER WOMAN
It's a long time since I've seen you
Listen
well
perhaps you could
well
come and visit me
come and see your old mother
now and then
yes that'd be good
you see I

THE DAUGHTER
Interrupts her
Yes
I thought I'd drop in
just briefly
just
to say hello
Short pause
yes I don't have much time
I've got to leave straight away

THE OLDER WOMAN
Do you have to leave already
You've just arrived
Couldn't you
Breaks off
It was good to see you
And
yes

THE DAUGHTER
Yes I just thought I'd drop in
as it were

But I've got to leave
straight away

THE OLDER WOMAN
Yes
well look after yourself
then
and we'll talk soon
I hope
Short pause
But listen
it's been a long time since I've seen you
It was really good to see you again
She and the Daughter move away from each other.
Calls to her
No don't go
You mustn't
The Friend comes walking towards the Daughter and they
stop, she looks at him, then looks away

THE DAUGHTER
He was there
and I didn't know him
Short pause
But then he was there in front of me
came towards me
he came walking towards me
from far away
towards me and towards me
he came
with his hair
And the rain in his hair
Short pause
And the light from his eyes
Short pause
Closer and closer
he came
and I could not

Breaks off
And then he was there in front of me

THE FRIEND
You mustn't meet me
This is not how it is
You mustn't
*The Daughter looks at the Older Man, and then she walks
towards him*

THE OLDER MAN
To the Daughter
Well hello
This is nice
It's been a long time since I've seen you
Quite short pause
Good of you to drop in

THE DAUGHTER
I thought I should
Seeing

THE OLDER MAN
And how are you

THE DAUGHTER
Good thanks
Everything's fine

THE OLDER MAN
That's good to hear
Short pause
This is so nice
Short pause
So everything's fine
then

THE DAUGHTER
A little uncertainly
Yes
Pause

THE OLDER MAN
> Well I'm glad you came
> really glad

THE DAUGHTER
> Yes
> I thought I should drop in

THE OLDER MAN
> That was kind
> of you
> *Pause*
> And you're alright
> then

THE DAUGHTER
> Not too bad

THE OLDER MAN
> Good to hear
> because you know
> well I worry about you
> you see
> yes
> of course I often think about you
> because it's not
> well not all that easy
> to be young

THE DAUGHTER
> I'm not all that young

THE OLDER MAN
> No not really young

THE DAUGHTER
> No I can't be
> *Teasing a little*
> not when I look at my father
> and see how old he's become

THE OLDER MAN
>Old and old
>Not too old to
>*Breaks off*

THE DAUGHTER
>Not too old
>you mean
>not too old to have
>a new girlfriend

THE OLDER MAN
>Yes
>*Attempts to ignore it*
>Oh well
>*Pause*

THE DAUGHTER
>You see each other often

THE OLDER MAN
>Yes we
>*Wants to tell her something, but hesitates*
>yes we
>we
>yes
>*Short pause*
>well
>we're thinking
>that perhaps we should
>well perhaps we should move in together

THE DAUGHTER
>But you're not going to marry her

THE OLDER MAN
>*Hesitates*
>No

THE DAUGHTER
> Getting married for the third time
> *Short pause*
> First my mother
> *Short pause*
> then that woman

THE OLDER MAN
> You never liked her

THE DAUGHTER
> No
> *Pause*
> And now a third one
> *Pause*
> Are you're going to marry her

THE OLDER MAN
> Well we might
> end up getting married

THE DAUGHTER
> Are you going to move
> to her place

THE OLDER MAN
> I might do that
> we'll see
> nothing's been decided
> Of course
> I want to stay here
> live in the same town as you

THE DAUGHTER
> Yes
> *Pause*
> But
> yes
> *Short pause, then quickly*
> well I'd better be going

THE OLDER MAN
    Are you doing something

THE DAUGHTER
    I've got an appointment

THE OLDER MAN
    Now tonight

THE DAUGHTER
    Yes
    well I just wanted to drop in
    and say hello
    when I happened to be on this side
    of town

THE OLDER MAN
    Oh
    I see
    Short pause
    Well it was good of you to drop in
    It's been a long time since I've seen you
    You have to come back soon

THE DAUGHTER
    I'll do that

THE OLDER MAN
    Yes
    Pause
    You must do that

THE DAUGHTER
    Is she coming soon
    your girlfriend

THE OLDER MAN
    Yes
    Short pause
    yes she's staying with me at the moment
    went out to do some shopping

THE DAUGHTER
She doesn't want to meet me

THE OLDER MAN
No it's not
Short pause
if you stay a little longer
you'll get to meet each other
Short pause
but it's not really
that easy
she feels
perhaps
well that perhaps it can wait
There's no rush

THE DAUGHTER
No
Short pause
I think I'll
Breaks off

THE OLDER MAN
Or you could meet each other later
that's probably just
as well
but
of course you could stay
It's time you get to meet each other
of course

THE DAUGHTER
I've got to meet someone

THE OLDER MAN
You're going out

THE DAUGHTER
Yes
Pause

THE OLDER MAN
> I see
> and then
> *Breaks off*

THE DAUGHTER
> What

THE OLDER MAN
> No nothing
> *The Daughter turns to leave and he follows her*
> Listen
> I've been thinking
> when you were a child
> is there something you remember
> something you remember better
> than anything else
> one thing that has remained with you
> *She continues to walk*
> well
> *Short pause*
> something that's there
> that's still in you
> something that's you
> that's part of your life
> *She doesn't turn around*
> well something that's good
> that fills you
> with joy
> or if not
> exactly that
> at least something
> well something you enjoy
> that makes life worth living
> something that
> *Breaks off*
> Why don't you stay for a while
> Do you have to leave already

You've just arrived
Why don't you stay here
just a little longer
Don't go yet
Can't we be together for a while
*He turns around, looks towards the Friend, then he looks
down, shyly*

THE DAUGHTER

No
She turns away from the Older Man. Long pause
And he came walking towards me
with rain in his hair
one night
he came walking towards me
Short pause
he came walking
in his very own light
Short pause
he came walking
in the music
that belongs to him
And the rain in his hair
will always be there
His hair in the rain
one night
just there
just then

THE OLDER WOMAN

She walked in the night
in the rain
in the wind

THE DAUGHTER

Most things change
vanish
become something else
but one thing that never changes

is rain in his hair
one night
just there
just then
*Short pause. The Older Man and the Older Woman look at
each other, they stand still, then look down*
He came walking towards me
And his hand that waves

THE OLDER WOMAN

She must have gone down to the harbour
walked along the quays

THE DAUGHTER

For his hair in the rain
is there
Short pause
like the light of heaven
Short pause
For love is like death
the way his hand
that waves
is always there too
His hair in the rain
And only one rainy night
*The Friend stretches his hands towards her and she walks
towards him and he welcomes her and they stand and hold
each other, and they let each other go, she walks away from
him and he stands and looks after her*

THE OLDER WOMAN

She walked along the quays
in the rain and the wind
in the dark
in the black dark

THE DAUGHTER

I see
Short pause

everything calms down
And nothing is as lucid
as pain
And rain in his hair

THE OLDER WOMAN
She kept walking along the quays
in the dark
alone
in the night

THE DAUGHTER
And from far away
he came walking towards me
in his very own light
Long pause. She and the Friend move away from each other
And in there
in the great luminous sleep
in that darkness
in that luminous darkness
we find
Short pause
we find the great joy
the joy of the great sleep

THE OLDER WOMAN
She walked there in the night
along the quays
in the dark
in the wind
she walked there alone
in the rain

THE FRIEND
To the Daughter
I can come to you

THE OLDER MAN
To the Daughter
why don't you come to me

be with me
talk to me

THE OLDER WOMAN
To the Daughter
Come to me
If you want to
you can live with me
I am there
I need you

THE OLDER MAN
To the Daughter
Can I help you
in any way
can I do something for you
Short pause
Come
talk to me
Be where I am

THE OLDER WOMAN
To the Daughter
Come to me
please
I care so much about you

THE FRIEND
To the Daughter
I can come to you
I am with you
we shall be together

THE DAUGHTER
I have to be alone

THE OLDER WOMAN
To the Daughter
You have to come to me
talk to me

THE DAUGHTER
To the Friend
But I miss you
The Friend walks towards her and she looks at him, afraid

THE FRIEND
You mustn't

THE DAUGHTER
You were
inside my heart
again
you were there

THE OLDER WOMAN
In the black night
she was walking along the quays
alone
in the dark

THE FRIEND
You mustn't come

THE OLDER WOMAN
And the waves
rolled and rolled against the quays
*The Daughter and the Friend look at each other, then they both
look down*

THE DAUGHTER
You will always stand there
in the rain
with your hair in the rain
and your hand waving
Pause
And it's so frightening
It's such a
great nothingness

THE FRIEND
But that's how it is
We can't choose

We are each other
We stand there in the rain

THE OLDER WOMAN
She walked along the quays
alone
in the night

THE DAUGHTER
But that's how it is
We are there
We stand there together
in the rain

THE FRIEND
We always stand there
And we never stand there
And it's good
and it hurts

THE DAUGHTER
Nods
Yes
Pause
Why is it like that

THE FRIEND
That's just how it is
Maybe
Long pause
And everything's a long time ago
and everything's just happened
And it doesn't matter
what we do
and what we don't do

THE DAUGHTER
For it rained
in your hair
And we'll never leave each other
That's just how it is

Short pause
And your hand
Waves to me
from far away
abandons solitude
and I go to the edge
and I stand there
and look out to the sea
until your hand
falls down upon me
and touches my hair
imperceptibly
like a dark night
And your hand strokes my hair

THE OLDER WOMAN
And then
well
well no one knows what happened

THE DAUGHTER
And your hand has never stroked my hair
and yet it does
so often
I feel your hand in my hair
And I stand there on the edge
I see your hand
I see your hand
I see that the dark sky
and the rain
are your hand
Pause
I want to hold your hand
*The Friend stretches his hand out towards her, and she stands
there, quite a distance from him, and he looks at his hand,
then he looks at her and they walk towards each other and they
stretch their hands towards each other and stand there and
hold each other's hands, they move their fingers in and out, tell
each other their stories with their fingers and after a while they*

*embrace and stand there holding each other and they hold each
other closely and calmly, and then they let each other go. They
embrace each other, kiss each other. Long pause*

THE OLDER WOMAN

They found her in the morning
floating in the sea
Short pause
She was floating in the sea
Long pause

THE YOUNG MAN

To the Young Woman
We'll manage
It'll be fine
you'll see
Pause

THE YOUNG WOMAN

Yes
Pause

THE FRIEND

I'll never come back
I'll always come back
Pause

THE OLDER MAN

To the Older Woman
And now you should go
I don't want to see you
I never want to see you again
Long pause

THE DAUGHTER

From far away
I shouldn't have done it
I want to live
I want to see the sea
I want to see the waves on the sea
I want to walk in the rain

in the wind
in the dark
I want to be with you
I didn't want to do it
But everything was black
and wet
He was black and wet
and luminous
Short pause
And the water
And the waves
The waves that rolled
Short pause
and rolled
and he was so good
he was peace
a peace as great as love
as calm as the sea
And the sky
was his hand
Short pause
But I didn't want to

THE OLDER WOMAN
To the Older Man
I'm leaving

THE OLDER MAN
I can't bear
to see your face

THE DAUGHTER
I regret it
I want to come back
I want to be alone again
I should not
Breaks off

Black